ESSAYS ON RUSSIAN INTELLECTUAL HISTORY

THE WALTER PRESCOTT WEBB MEMORIAL LECTURES: V

THE WALTER PRESCOTT WEBB MEMORIAL LECTURES

ESSAYS ON RUSSIAN INTELLECTUAL HISTORY

BY

JOSEPH T. FUHRMANN

EDWARD C. BOCK

LEON I. TWAROG

Foreword by James P. Hart

Introduction by Sidney Monas

Edited by
Leon Borden Blair

PUBLISHED FOR THE UNIVERSITY OF TEXAS AT ARLINGTON
BY THE UNIVERSITY OF TEXAS PRESS, AUSTIN & LONDON

International Standard Book Number 0-292-70119-5
Library of Congress Catalog Card Number 75-155640
© 1971 by The University of Texas at Arlington
All Rights Reserved
Manufactured in the United States of America

FOREWORD

The lectures included in this volume relate to subjects outside the particular area of historical study in which Walter Prescott Webb specialized and wrote. That does not mean, however, that the topics discussed would not have interested him. He wrote about what he knew best, because it was a part of the atmosphere in which he had lived as well as because he gave it thoughtful study and thorough research. On the other hand, no part of history would have failed to excite his interest, especially when it relates, as these lectures do, to a powerful nation that unavoidably will play a major part in shaping the future for everybody on earth.

It is not my purpose, however, to discuss the lectures, but to write a few words about Dr. Webb as I knew him personally. Walter Prescott Webb was not an easy man to know. He had a natural reserve and dignity that protected his valued privacy and personal integrity. Also, he was inherently modest, remembering, I believe, that nothing that he achieved had been accomplished except through long hard work.

That is not to say that he lacked confidence or the courage to stand firm for what he thought was right and important. Having made up his mind on what he considered a critical issue, he was outspoken and unshakable. Unavoidably he made enemies, some of whom were influential in determining his professional future. But he never swerved or backed up; and in the end some whom he had opposed were even moved to recommend him for the highest academic rank that his university then conferred. It is a matter of enduring gratification to me that as Chancellor of The University of Texas I had some part in seeing that this recommendation was approved and that Dr. Webb got the recognition he deserved.

His austerity was not, however, the side of his nature that was always dominant. I have heard stories told by some of his friends about his relaxing around the camp fire or the poker table. I did not share those experiences; but Mrs. Hart and I did have some delightful evenings with him at the Headliners Club when we chanced to meet him and invited him to join us. His conversation was lively and witty, as well as wise; in short, he was good company.

Personally, I must also acknowledge gratefully his steadfast and generous friendship when, for me, the political winds were overwhelmingly adverse. He did not look back then, either. It was truly an honor and inspiration to have known him.

JAMES P. HART

PREFACE

The fifth annual Walter Prescott Webb Memorial Lectures, held in Texas Hall on the campus of The University of Texas at Arlington, April 9, 1970, dealt with some aspects of modern Russian intellectual life. In the morning sessions Professors Joseph T. Fuhrmann and Edward C. Bock discussed the work of the philosophers Gregorii Savvich Skovoroda and Vladimir Soloviev. The evening lecture by Professor Leon I. Twarog, chairman of the Department of Slavic Languages and Literatures at Ohio State University, traced the history of literary censorship in nineteenth- and twentieth-century Russia.

Walter Prescott Webb was interested in new ideas. He encouraged scholars to find areas where their experience gave them unique insight and knowledge. Although his untimely death precluded personal investigation into Russian history, he recognized the need, and he urged others to explore its many aspects. These lectures then, on Russian intellectual history, are in the Webb tradition.

Transliterations always present problems, as in these essays, when several authorities are writing and are not available for verification of or acquiescence in editorial changes. I therefore have supplied a consistent transliteration for names which appear in more than one essay.

LEON BORDEN BLAIR

CONTENTS

INTRODUCTION

Russian intellectual history has been very largely a history of the
intelligentsia. It is generally acknowledged to have been poor in
original ideas, but rich in heroes and vivid personalities, dense
with a living, proliferating relationship between political realities and the power of ideas and ideals to transform them. It is a
history of absorption and adaptation, of what came to Russia
from outside, and of what Russians made of it in the special
conditions governing their lives. The three following essays are
in that context.

It is customary to regard the intelligentsia—that "spiritual
brotherhood" of the Russian Enlightenment, as Ivanov-Razumnik
called it—as the product of a conflict between Western philosophical, political, and social ideals and Russian political, social,
and economic realities. If we are forced to admit that the realities
were rather grim, we must also affirm that the ideals were
staunchly and heroically held. The Russians always contributed
a special human intensity, a fervor, warmth, and sincerity to any
idea they embraced. They had a tendency, it is true, to push
things too far, to draw the most radical conclusions, and not only
to draw them but to try to live them; the provisional, tentative
nature of much of the Western thought they absorbed was lost to

them. Yet in this very extremism, this radicalism of thought, this intellectual fervor and sincerity and dedication, lies the special contribution of the Russian intelligentsia to Western civilization. They were, in a sense, its acid test.

I referred above to the Russian Enlightenment. It took place roughly between 1830 and 1900, a century later than its European counterpart; like the European Enlightenment, it contained within itself a countermovement, an antienlightenment, a Romantic reaction against that process of secularization for which the word *enlightenment* is an abbreviation and a euphemism. Along with the attempt to unveil, demystify, desacralize, take the magic out of (and thus inevitably undermine) the old religious and political authorities, along with the attempt to establish reason and empirical knowledge and ethical common sense as the new authorities, there was also a search for substitute religions and substitute beliefs—nationalism, socialism, art, and, not least by any means, science itself. Trend and countertrend blended and shared a common atmosphere. What Herzen said of Westernizers and Slavophiles—that they were a Janus head, facing in opposite directions but sharing a common trunk—may be applied as well (though taking into account a sharper antagonism) to the scientism and antiscientism of the whole Russian Enlightenment, of which the Westernizer-Slavophile controversy was an important part. The language, the tone, the atmosphere, and the psychology by and in which the intelligentsia lived throughout the nineteenth century drew heavily on the traditions and vocabulary and experience of the old religion.

The European Enlightenment, too, had its roots in religious experience. Carl Becker, in *The Heavenly City of the Eighteenth Century Philosophers*, has demonstrated the range of religious aspirations and values held by the *philosophes* and translated and transposed into secular terminology, terms used by the most ardently atheistic or coldly agnostic among them. Robert Palmer on the other hand has shown, in *Catholics and Unbelievers in Eighteenth Century France*, the extent to which the Catholic Church, and more specifically, the Jesuit order, was involved, at an early date, in the project of the Encyclopedia; in other words, that a good deal that was central to Enlightenment thinking emerged directly from the Church itself, before authorities within the Church lost their nerve. If French Catholicism influenced the specific forms that the Enlightenment took in France, Lutheranism certainly played an enormous role in the thought of the Enlightenment in Germany, and Anglicanism in England. In studying Russia, however, most historians have tended to neglect the role of the Russian Church or of its religious traditions and general atmosphere in the formation of the intelligentsia.

That is not entirely and absolutely true, of course. It was Vladimir Soloviev, alerted perhaps by his friend and mentor, Dostoevsky, who first pointed out the religious passion and exaltation with which the intelligentsia preached its scientistic secularism. He suggested that its motto might appropriately have read: "Man is descended from the apes; therefore, we must love one another." Indeed the religious tone of the "men of the sixties and seventies" has often been noted, though rarely examined and analyzed. It has been noted, too, that such outstanding leaders of the radical intelligentsia as Chernyshevsky and Dobroliubov were *popovtsy*, sons of Orthodox clergy. Franco Venturi has pointed out that Chernyshevsky's father was an unusually well educated man, that Chernyshevsky's precocious early education took place in his father's library, which included an extraordinary and extraordinarily tolerant array of books, including Voltaire and the *philosophes*. It is clear that the standard notion of the provincial Russian clergy as ignorant, superstitious, and illiterate as well as intolerant needs at least to be seriously modified.[1] We know also that such revolutionaries as Shchapov and Kelsiev, who hoped to tap a great potential revolutionary source in the discontent and oppression of the Old Believers, found that the further they made their way into the intellectual and spiritual world of the Old Believers the more attractively familiar it seemed; Shchapov ended as a learned historian of the religious schism, Kelsiev as himself an Old Believer![2] Most prominently, of course, Nicholas Berdiaev has emphasized the close if antag- onistic relation between Russian religious and secular thought. Berdiaev has had a considerable impact and influence on religious thought in the West, but our historians of Russian thought have by and large reacted against this man who began his book, *The Russian Idea*, with the following statement: "What will interest me in the following pages is not so much the question: what has Russia been from the empirical point of view, as the question: what was the thought of the Creator about Russia?" In spite of his identifying himself with the Creator, it is time, nevertheless, for a serious reappraisal of Berdiaev's work.

We have, as well, a number of books that deal seriously and, some of them, like Father Florovsky's *Puti russkoi bogoslovii*,

[1] Franco Venturi, *Roots of Revolution* (New York: Alfred A. Knopf, 1960), pp. 129–133.

[2] Ibid., pp. 114, 187–203; V. I. Kelsiev, "*Ispoved'*," ed. E. Kingisepp, introduction by M. Klevenskii, in *Literaturnoe Nasledstvo*, nos. 41 and 42 (1941): 253 ff.; A. P. Shchapov, *Sochineniia*, 3 vols. (St. Petersburg, 1906–1908); *Neizdannye sochineniia*, ed. E. I. Chernyshev (Kazan, 1927).

exhaustively with the overtly religious thought of otherwise secular thinkers. But there has been no important study dealing
with the intellectual atmosphere of Orthodox Christianity in
Russia, with the Russian religious mind of the eighteenth and
the first half of the nineteenth centuries. That such a study is
badly needed springs instantly to mind when we consider the
lives and works of Gregory Skovoroda and Vladimir Soloviev,
both of them religious philosophers rather than members of the
intelligentsia, yet of obvious importance in the history of Russian
thought.

Skovoroda died at the end of the eighteenth century, before
the intelligentsia had come into being, and Soloviev, premature-
ly, at the end of the nineteenth, as the intelligentsia was entering
its last, twilit, apocalyptic phase which he did so much to influence and shape. Between them they frame the era of militant
secularization that I have called the Russian Enlightenment, and
because both were profoundly religious men and steeped in their
native religious tradition, while at the same time strongly "Westernized," not merely in the somewhat snobbish sense of being
au courant with what was going on in Europe, but in the sense
of having a strong secular bent, a need to reconcile what they
felt to be the truths of revealed religion with the truths of
rational-empirical inquiry, the truths of philosophy, they may
inspire a more balanced view of the relationship between traditional Russian religion and the Russian Enlightenment.

Grigorii Savvich Skovoroda, as Mr. Fuhrmann eloquently outlines his life and work, is an enormously appealing and attractive
figure. But also enigmatic. With regard to his intellect: Where
did it come from? What was its main thrust? With regard
to his place in intellectual history: What influence did he have?

In what context does he belong? Wherever we place him, he
begins to bristle with paradoxes—a rationalist who speaks in
the language of revelation; a man of calm inner peace who spent
his life in restless wandering; a skeptic and a questioner who
affirms the authority of the Church; a pantheist, but Orthodox;
a Westerner whose thought closely resembles much of the neo-
stoicism of the eighteenth century, yet who is so absolutely
archetypically Russian in the style of his thought and life; a
strannik, or holy wanderer, with the mind of Socrates and the
temperament of Avvakum!

These, and other questions that Skovoroda suggests can be
raised, but cannot be settled, here, any more than the problem
of the Russian religious mind in its penultimate phase can be
settled. Yet some of the questions are worth dwelling on and
teasing a bit. The question of influence, for instance.

I once heard it said that "influence" was basically an astrologi-
cal, not an empirical, conception, and I am often inclined to
agree with this. Where many historians write "influence" they
mean confluence or convergence. Nevertheless, there is such a
thing. People work on other people. The question is how and in
what way. It is often a question of one man's inner need finding
some outer objectification or projection. Edward Brown has
written a monograph on Nicholas Stankevich, attempting to
prove that Stankevich's influence was merely the product of the
need for it, as felt by the more gifted members of his circle.[3]
There is something to this, but not everything. We too often
think of influence in purely bookish terms, in terms of one man's
reading what another has written and finding that the latter's ar-

[3] Edward J. Brown, *Stankevich and his Moscow Circle, 1830–1840*
(Stanford: Stanford University Press, 1966).

ticulation or solution of certain problems advances his own
thinking in this regard. Influence is, certainly, more mysterious
and less rational than that. And Russia has been for ages, and
still is, a country of underground influences, of influences that
cannot be traced through the written word. Skovoroda's works
were not published until long after his death, and he was not read
much before the twentieth century, but what was the influence
of the *Igor Tale*? What was the influence of the *Autobiography*
of the Archpriest Avvakum? Or of Radishchev's *Journey*? Writers like Chaadaev, Abram Tertz, and Amalrik found it very
difficult to present their writings in open, public circulation.
Their influence is unfathomable, immeasurable, but unquestion-
ably they have had influence.

In the case of Skovoroda, there are hints. Legends about him
and his life persisted in the Ukraine; the fact, recorded by Mr.
Bock, that Soloviev's mother was a Skovoroda and that family
tradition was strong (one is often reminded, as in the case of
Chaadaev and the Slavophiles, of the extraordinarily close family
relations that web Russian intellectual history); the striking re-
semblance to him of the late Leo Tolstoy, though this may be
coincidence. In any case, as a figure, a "literary portrait" (to use
Rosanov's phrase), this holy cossack would seem to belong not
at the periphery but close to the center of Russian intellectual
history.

There is also the question of the influences which bore upon
him. He was educated in the formal sense at the Kiev Theological Academy, informally at the court of the Empress Elizabeth,
and at a number of universities and cities in the West, though
it is far from certain which ones, or what he learned there. We
know that the Kiev Academy played an enormous role in what

is called the Westernization of Russia. A number of high authorities in the Russian clergy were educated there in the seventeenth century and early eighteenth—from the Patriarch Nikon
who reformed the books and provoked the great church schism
to Theophan Prokopovich who hymned praises to the secular
state of Peter the Great. A source of Latin learning and a slender
but important link by way of Poland with the humanism of the
Western Renaissance, the academy was the most important seat
of higher education in Russia until well into the second half of
the eighteenth century. But it has been little studied—as, indeed,
the life, education, and social and intellectual climate surrounding the Russian clergy in general have been little studied.[4] We
know that Skovoroda learned Latin and Greek and Hebrew there,
the sacred languages. But what did he read, say, in Greek? Did
he read Plotinus? The Gnostics? Plato? And in what light did
he read them? Were his rationalist allegorizations of Holy Writ
original with him or were they the common language of a small
group of enlightened spirits at the academy?

Mr. Fuhrmann is surely right to stress the Church's tolerance
toward Skovoroda, and Skovoroda's wish to remain within the
folds of Orthodoxy. The Orthodox Church, as Dostoevsky and
Berdiaev insisted, and as most of us have been reluctant to believe, was rather a liberal institution with regard to religious
thought, with the exception of a few brief reactionary periods.
The excommunication of Tolstoy in 1902 was, after all, an

---

[4] More or less standard reading on the subject are the amusing "seminary sketches" of N. G. Pomialovskii; these, however, are apt to be
somewhat misleading. N. G. Pomialovskii, *Ocherki bursa* (St. Petersburg, 1865). These sketches deal, in any case, with the nineteenth century, not with the eighteenth.

extraordinary event, extraordinarily provoked; and the period of
the Metropolitan Filaret, a reaction against the wild religious
liberalism of the time of Alexander I. Since Skovoroda made no
attempt to publish his writings during his lifetime, I do not
speak here of ecclesiastical censorship, which could no doubt be
crude and arbitrary, but rather of the tolerance of known beliefs.
In any case, I believe Mr. Fuhrmann underestimates somewhat
the degree to which Skovoroda required tolerating. Not only
did his tendency to equate Nature with God suggest a most
heretical pantheism, but his philosopher's quest—the pursuit of
happiness—differed radically from the religious quest, which is
to find God. Now, the idea of the pursuit of happiness, and the
idea of Nature as fundamentally orderly, "balanced," and just,
were certainly two of the most important ideas of the Western
Enlightenment; but they have their origins in Greek speculative
thought and are as ancient as Western civilization itself. They
comprise, however, the philosopher's way, not the way of the
prophet; the way of Job's friends, not the way of Job. "God
does not ask the impossible," says the philosopher. "God asks
only the impossible," says the prophet. Leo Shestov, a great critic
of the last days of the Russian intelligentsia, has seen these two
ways as fundamentally at war with each other from the very beginning of Christianity—Athens vs. Jerusalem, speculation vs.
revelation.[5] I would only like to add that the conflict existed in
ancient Judaism as well as in early Christianity and cannot simply
be attributed, in the manner of Shestov, to the Greeks. The pro-
phetic tradition and the rabbinical have always viewed each other

[5] These are the titles of Shestov's last two books. Leo Shestov, *Athens
and Jerusalem* (Athens: Ohio University Press, 1966); *Umozrenie i
otkrovenie* (Paris: YMCA Press, 1964).

with a certain uneasy tension. In other words, the conflict, real as it is, certainly need not be viewed as one of East vs. West, nor need it be assumed that all tendencies to rational speculation entered Russia from Western Europe. We may well be dealing here with a development common to all Christian cultures, a far weaker growth in Russia, no doubt, where there was no Renaissance and no Age of Reason, but one already well under way there by the mid-seventeenth century, and one which therefore welcomed eagerly unto itself more fully blown and better-articulated models from abroad from that time on. Skovoroda in any case impels us to look hard at the native tradition of religious thought we have hitherto assiduously avoided.

Skovoroda lived at a time when what was recognizably native in Russian culture was also distinctly religious and even churchly. A century later, when what was considered cultivated or cultured in Russia was completely secularized, the Russian intelligentsia seemed to be moving in the direction of intense scientism and materialism, whether of a socialist or liberal cast. Religious life seemed to be moving toward mere administrative churchliness, handmaiden to the regime's reactionary conservatism which was, in its own way, equally materialistic. Soloviev tried to reverse this tendency. He was enormously influential. Single-handedly he created a lay theology and produced disciples like Berdiaev and Sergei Bulgakov. He had an enormous impact on the symbolist movement in poetry—on Blok, Belyi, and on Viacheslav Ivanov. His spirit hovered over the publication of *Vekhi* in 1909 and the probings into the life and origins of the Russian intelligentsia undertaken by one of the *Vekhi* authors, M. O. Gershenzon. Because he brought to his task a mastery of formal, systematic philosophy, as developed in the West, he was hailed as the first great Russian philosopher, possibly the only one.

Yet as a formal philosopher Soloviev strikes me today as rather uninteresting—a neo-Schellingian of great range and some philosophical eloquence, but unoriginal and fundamentally dated. It is as a culture-hero, a mystic, and a poet that Soloviev is truly interesting. As a typical member of the intelligentsia, while at the same time its most severe critic, Soloviev engaged his entire personality in a political struggle on behalf of Russian culture. As a mystic and poet, his vision was constantly at war with his thought, from the appearance before him in (of all places!) the British Museum of a beautiful woman beckoning him to Egypt, to the vision of Apocalypse and Antichrist that he describes in his last book, *Three Conversations*. Here the figure of Antichrist, ostensibly uttering the opinions of Leo Tolstoy, actually expresses many of Soloviev's former ideas and speculative tendencies as well—as Leo Shestov, in his excellent essay on Soloviev, has pointed out.[6]

Soloviev's father was the first great Russian scientific historian, the Russian Ranke, a most learned Westernizer. To this day his history of Russia is fundamental to any serious study of the subject. His mother was a Skovoroda, and his grandfather on his father's side a devout priest who greatly influenced his childhood. As a young man, Soloviev was exposed to the best Russian minds of his time. Dostoevsky was enchanted with him, and modeled the character of Aliosha Karamazov after him. Constantine Leontiev, who at first adored him, later denounced him as Satan and

[6] L. Shestov, "Umozrenie i Apokolipsis," in *Umozrenie i otkrovenie*, pp. 23–92.

Antichrist, because he felt that Soloviev like Dostoevsky had suc-
cumbed to what he called "rosewater Christianity," the illusion
that it was possible to establish the kingdom of God on this
earth, fundamentally the same illusion (in Leontiev's view) as
that which held the materialist intelligentsia in thrall. Soloviev,
on the other hand, with typical generosity, wrote on the occasion
of Leontiev's death a most warm and glowing tribute to that odd
man who had tried to reconcile within himself the qualities of a
rapacious esthete and an ascetic monk.

Like Cardinal Newman, Soloviev had a religious experience
early. Yet he also had his period of doubt and atheism. True, it
was atypical for his time, and impelled his precocious mind to
Schopenhauer and Spinoza rather than to the more fashionable
materialist atheism of his day. Soloviev came back to religion;
yet his religious convictions remained somewhat divided between a need to demonstrate, like Skovoroda, that the orderliness
and conformity of Nature demonstrated the existence of a phi-
losopher-God who did not ask the impossible, and the vision of
the prophet who saw God as precisely a violation of the laws of
Nature, a God of miracles for whom all things were possible.

For a time, Soloviev was a Catholicizer within the Orthodox
Church, but only for a time, and unlike Newman, it was never
the problem of historical authority, apostolic succession and the
primacy of Peter, that concerned him the most. I believe Mr.
Bock reads Soloviev as more of a Roman Catholic than I do, but
in any case I would submit that his interests were ecumenical—
the reunification of the churches, the re-creation of the Church
as a single body, and through this single Church, the unification
of mankind. In this Soloviev most resembles and was most influenced by Chaadaev, who regularly took Communion in both

churches but never left the one into which he had been born. Like Chaadaev at the time of the writing of the *Apologie d'un fou* (c. 1837), Soloviev believed that Russia had, with regard to the history of mankind, an unfulfilled destiny; like Chaadaev he was austere and restrained in his notion of what Russia had accomplished toward that destiny, and also like Chaadaev he hoped much for the future of his country. But he had also gone to school to the Slavophiles who had reacted against Chaadaev, and although he had a far more positive and elaborate notion than they of the state's role in its relationship to society, he nevertheless owes much to them for his concept of a Christian Society.

Soloviev's concept is at the same time visionary and rationalistic. Like T. S. Eliot, who also formulated *The Idea of a Christian Society*, he denied that his work was in any way utopian. He saw it, he said, as a practical blueprint that accepted the weak, the fallible, the fallen nature of man. He set up, as his figures of authority in this Platonic but nonutopian commonwealth, an emperor, priests, and prophets—as though along with kingship and priesthood one could institutionalize prophecy! As a very astute critic, R. P. Blackmur, wrote of Eliot, one might say also of Soloviev: "If God is not already in first place, as well as in all other places, then to put him there is to put him out of reach."[7] But of course there is one important difference: Eliot wrote for a society which, though it still had an established church, was so clearly and thoroughly secular in its outlook as to induce Eliot to anticipate the charge of utopianism. Soloviev's society with its established church was almost as thoroughly secularized. But

---

[7] R. P. Blackmur, *The Expense of Greatness* (New York: Arrow Editions, 1940; reprinted, Magnolia, Mass.: Peter Smith, Publisher, 1969), p. 240.

neither the church nor the state of which it was a part would admit it. As their authority became increasingly precarious, both sought to maintain a cumbersome, inefficient, ineffective apparatus of censorship and repression, to try, to some degree, to prevent people from saying too destructively that the magic had indeed gone. Soloviev's idea of a Christian order was much more likely to be taken seriously as a criticism of the church and state that actually existed in Russia than was Eliot's of church and state in England!

In the Anglo-American context, Eliot's views appeared as conservative, indeed almost reactionary. Those same views, elaborated by Soloviev—to be sure in a more thorough, more systematic, but also more archaic, more nineteenth-century manner, in the very context of the Russian theocracy reinforced by censorship and a police state—appeared as strikingly liberal, libertarian, and almost radical. We cannot escape the conviction that censorship has been a great shaping force in Russian thought and literature. But censorship is a complex question; we must try to avoid the danger of being glib about it.

Censorship is a form of repression. Repression, both Marx and Freud tell us, is the consequence of division and conflict, whether of classes or of psychic energies. Every state is repressive, and every society exercises some sort of censorship, just as does every individual over his own thoughts. Still, the history of Russia during the last century and a half has been one of unusually harsh repression. Russia did not pay for its harshness by collapse into chaos and ineffectuality, or by loss of its position as a great power. The society and the organic state survived its chaotic interludes.

Certainly, censorship and repression have been closely related to cataclysmic social changes, and the relationship has been not a simple but a dialectical one. We must confront the paradox, however, that Russia, which suffered the most severe censorship in the world between 1825 and 1925, also produced the world's greatest literature during that period; that Pushkin, who personally suffered untold agonies at the hands of both the ordinary censors and the censorship tutelage of Nicholas I, nevertheless produced (in the abbreviated Academy edition) ten very solid volumes of work, the sum of which is the greatest poetry of the nineteenth century, and two or three pieces of its most brilliant prose. Did the censorship diminish or augment his talent? Did it diminish or augment Soloviev's work?

Both Nietzsche and Leontiev insisted that suffering lived through, suffering genuinely experienced and absorbed, always augmented, never diminished talent. But repression is suffering that is not allowed to surface, suffering incomplete, so to speak. For censorship as it was practiced in Russia before the time of Stalin, one can only say that it was singularly unsuccessful in repressing what it seemed intent on repressing, and that the attendant suffering caused to artists and critics and public, while one would hardly dare to try to justify it on these grounds, nevertheless did enhance, did lend a certain stature and nobility of the kind that Nietzsche said came from suffering, to the literary life of the Russian nineteenth century.

Of course, Mr. Twarog, in his excellent essay on censorship, does tend to exaggerate a little the intensity and efficiency with which the censors operated. True, the laws and the administration were at their most rigid during the period of Nicholas I. But Benckendorff was a rather inert, absentminded, slightly corrupt, fundamentally good-natured man. He did not conceive his mission in cosmic terms, to put it mildly. He was not a very admirable man, but in certain situations corrupt mediocrities of little energy are preferable to their sterner, more talented counterparts. The censorship of the old regime was, furthermore, in spite of occasional statements to the contrary, a fundamentally negative censorship; certain things could not be said, and there was an attempt (not very successful, to be sure) to specify in law and decree what these things were, to spell out the prison, so to speak. Since, as Stendhal once said, the man in jail who wants to get out has every advantage over his jailer who wants to keep him in, because he has ten times the motive, writers always had a basic inner, moral advantage over their censors, and it was one which, despite all the personal suffering and sorrow that resulted, they exercised successfully.

After the triumph of Stalin, the upheaval of collectivization and industrialization, the emergence of the doctrine of Socialist Realism, and the nightmare period of the great purges, the situation altered drastically. Roman Jakobson has spoken of "a generation that sacrificed its poets." The enormous flowering of Russian poetry and Russian painting and Russian music that characterized the period between 1913 and 1924 came to an end in the lethal climate of Stalinism. Poets committed suicide, or they died in Siberia, or they were shot, or they languished in emigration. Certainly the period between 1934 and 1956 was the bleakest and least inspiring period in Russian literature since the Mongol Yoke. (And one should remember that the time of the Mongol Yoke was a great period in Russian icon-painting!) Still, we now know that a number of masterpieces were produced during this period, even if they remained in dark corners or in desk drawers. Little by little now, the works of Mikhail Bulgakov,

Andrei Platonov, and Evgeny Schwartz are being published. We know also that such great writers as Pasternak and Mandelstam, Zabolotsky, and Akhmatova, although little or nothing of theirs was published during this period, went on writing. We know that the painter Filonov went on working and that about a hundred of his canvases are in the air-conditioned vaults of the Hermitage awaiting the day when they can be shown. All these works smell of tragedy and suffering; they seem, today, of a stature and richness that despair alone could have produced.

While it is merely a liberal prejudice, therefore, to think that freedom of expression and the flowering of literary culture are inextricably linked, it is nevertheless true that repression and censorship can reach a point that is almost total, a point at which literary culture is virtually wiped out.

Yet virtually is not completely, and even total, as in totalitarian, is only a figure of speech. No voice is wholly lost, and it would seem that in one form or another the repressed always returns. After the death of Stalin, we have seen in Russia the reemergence of a religious culture, an intelligentsia enchanted and intrigued not so much by the Orthodox Church as by the intellectual and spiritual tradition of Skovoroda, Soloviev, Berdiaev, and Shestov. In intellectual circles "God" is no longer a dirty word. Even among those who claim not to be religious, the almond eyes of the ancient icons exercise their potent charm. Along with the reemergence of religion, there is once again an underground press—a flourishing literature, some good, some bad, but much of it vital, distributed by what is called "self-publication" or *samizdat*.

Repression has not disappeared, nor has censorship. On the contrary, they are very severe, and writers have suffered much these last few years. But, more and more, censorship seems to be coming to resemble the fumbling, insecure, uneven, corrupt, and negative censorship of the period of Nicholas I and less the total obliteration, based on the power and self-confidence of the regime, of the time of Stalin.

The present is, of course, always arguable; and the future may well prove me wrong. But so, at the moment, it seems to me; and in this way, it seems to me, the papers included in this volume illuminate indirectly the current situation in the USSR.

SIDNEY MONAS

Austin, Texas

ESSAYS ON RUSSIAN INTELLECTUAL HISTORY

The First Russian Philosopher's Search
For the Kingdom of God

JOSEPH T. FUHRMANN

What is life? It is a journey; I strike out upon the road, not know-ing where I go or why."[1]

Grigorii Savvich Skovoroda

ACCORDING TO TRADITION the essay and the formal lecture are similar in that each permits its author moderately discursive expo-sition from a rather personal point of view without entitling the reader (or listener) to expect complete treatment of the subject. The titles of works in these genres may be suggestive rather than indicative, and for this I am especially grateful, since I should despair of capturing an audience's attention by announcing in advance that my topic is Grigorii Savvich Skovoroda, a Ukrainian-Russian mystic and wanderer of the eighteenth century. This is no reflection upon Skovoroda himself, merely a commentary

---

[1] Quoted in V. V. Zenkovsky, *A History of Russian Philosophy*, trans. George L. Kline, 2 vols. (New York: Columbia University Press; Lon-don: Routledge and Kegan Paul, 1953) I, 56. The Russian quote is in N. Stelletskii, "Stranstvuiushchii ukrainskii filosof Grigorii Savvich Skovoroda" [Wandering Ukrainian philosopher Grigorii Savvich Sko-voroda], *Trudy Kievskoi Dukhovnoi Akademii* [Works of the Kiev The-ological Academy] 2 (August 1894): 616.

upon the extent to which he has been appreciated by students of Russian intellectual history in the Soviet Union and abroad. In his own land a better than adequate edition of his work was not published until 1961. Fewer than fifty pages of his work are available in English translation, and I know of none in French or German. Furthermore, "no good studies of Skovoroda's thought exist in the English language, and very few have been attempted in *any* language."[2] My title, then, seeks to engage the reader's concern by stating the significance of our subject in order to understand the origins of philosophy in Russia. Before Skovoroda, Russian reflection on ultimate questions was oriented almost exclusively around traditional theological precepts and religious certainties, with a Christian adaptation of certain elements of Platonic and Aristotelian thought. Skovoroda extended the base of existing Russian thought by building, quite apart from the authority of the Church, a system of ideas partially indebted to an independent and broader analysis of the original sources of Greek and Roman philosophy. For this reason Skovoroda stands forth as the first true Russian philosopher.[3]

[2] We must thank George L. Kline and James M. Edie for these selections, which include valuable passages from M. I. Kovalinskii's *Life* of Skovoroda (see footnote 7 below). Kline's quote (with Zenkovsky's original emphasis) is from James M. Edie et al., eds. and trans., *Russian Philosophy*, 3 vols. (Chicago: Quadrangle Books, 1965) I: 14. Vladimir Ern's book on Skovoroda's life and thought (see footnote 5 below) is still of great value, as is Domet Oljančyn, *Hryhorij Skoworoda, 1722–1794; Der ukrainische Philosoph des xviii. Jahrhunderts und seine geistig-kulturelle Umwelt* (Berlin, 1928). The fairly recent date of Oljančyn's book makes his bibliography of studies on Skovoroda rather comprehensive.

[3] A secular culture arose in Russia somewhat before Skovoroda, but its representatives (Mikhail Lomonosov, Vasilii Tatishchev, and Nikolai

But if it is possible to speak of Skovoroda representing a *"secularization within the ecclesiastical consciousness,"* it is important to emphasize that Skovoroda did not break with the Church.[4] He sought the "kingdom of God" in the sense of seeing man's highest goal to be the rejection of worldly riches and ambitions and the attainment of inner peace through self-understanding and love of God.

Skovoroda, then, is a religious philosopher, and the Church's ability to produce him, as well as the compulsion he felt to remain within its institutional framework, should hint at the need to review critically our image of the Russian Church as an institution

---

Novikov, among others), while possessing philosophical viewpoints, did not consider themselves professional "philosophers," nor is the modern reader likely to find them significant if he reads them for philosophical content.

It is true, of course, that the "Russian" philosopher Skovoroda was actually Ukrainian by birth, residence, and immediate area of influence. By the late eighteenth century, however, the integration of the Ukraine into the cultural life of the Russian empire had gone so far that Skovoroda himself chose to write in Russian, with numerous letters in Latin and Greek, and this placed him, ultimately, within the overall framework of Russian history and culture. Moreover, although Skovoroda loved the Ukraine as his home, I find in him few elements of Ukrainian "nationalism," nor, for that matter, dissatisfaction in being a "Russian subject." Apparently, Skovoroda did not write in Ukrainian (not even in letters to fellow Ukrainians!), although one scholar has justly noted the difficulty presented to readers by Skovoroda's "terrible mixture of Church language with simple Ukrainian [speech], varied Polish words and many Belorussian provincialisms, and also Greek and Latin expressions." (Khidzheu, "Grigorii Varsava [*sic*] Skovoroda. Istoriko-kriticheskii ocherk," [Grigorii Skovoroda. An historical-critical study], *Teleskop* [Telescope] 26 (1835): 17 n.)

[4] Zenkovsky, *History of Russian Philosophy*, I, 45. (Emphasis from the original.)

lacking intellectual vitality or creativity by the time of Catherine the Great. True, many spiritually motivated, educated Russians were breaking with the Orthodox Church during the last third of the eighteenth century. But Skovoroda, the most learned Russian of the period,[5] was not in their number, a fact of some significance.

Skovoroda's sturdy independence and love of freedom might well have stemmed in part from the ethos of his homeland, the Ukraine, which had been but recently united to serfbound, autocratic Russia at the time of his birth in 1722. The area in which Skovoroda grew to young manhood retained many elements of a bold, wild, heroic past,[6] and regardless of how far his later wanderings carried him from his birthplace, the Ukraine was ever-prominent in Grigorii's mind.[7] His family, too, may have helped to instill in the boy a sense of robust individualism. The father, Savva Skovoroda, was a cossack in the town of Chernukhakh of the Kiev district,[8] an upright small landowner noted for his honesty and good character.

From the time he was seven, Grigorii inclined toward religious studies, music, and the sciences and displayed, as a student, a resolute spirit.[9] He loved to attend church. He sang in the

[5] V. Ern, *Grigorii Savvich Skovoroda, zhizn' i uchenie* [Grigorii Savvich Skovoroda: Life and teachings] (Moscow, 1912), p. 48.

[6] Ibid., p. 44.

[7] Kovalinskii tells us that Skovoroda "was accustomed to calling Little Russia his mother, and the Ukraine his aunt." See M. I. Kovalinskii, "Zhizn' Grigoriia Skovorody," [Life of Grigorii Skovoroda], reprinted in Grigorii Skovoroda, *Tvori v dvokh tomakh* [Works in two volumes] (Kiev, 1961), II: 511.

[8] Ibid., p. 488. Some authors incorrectly identify Savva as a priest (e.g., Khidzheu, "Grigorii Skovoroda," p. 18).

[9] Kovalinskii, "Zhizn' Grigoriia Skovorody," p. 488.

choir and did so with great skill. Skovoroda's parents customarily gave him much latitude, although his father, having at least modest means, wanted the boy to attend the famous Theological Academy at Kiev.[10] Skovoroda entered this school at the age of sixteen, but, being an excellent singer, he was soon sent to the court chapel at St. Petersburg to serve the Empress Elizabeth, a lady much dedicated to the beauties of Ukrainian music.[11] After two years, Skovoroda gained permission to return to his studies at Kiev. The education he received there was excellent, for the place and time, including even mathematics and some of the natural sciences.[12] Skovoroda's command of Latin and Greek is displayed in numerous, lengthy letters, and he learned Hebrew in order that he might be able to read the Hebraic-language editions of the Old Testament. Grigorii's most impressive learning, however, was in the areas of philosophy and theology. Here his readings ranged from Plato[13] and other Greek philosophers[14] to

[10] This academy had been founded a century earlier by Peter Mogila, a "Westernized" Eastern Orthodox scholar, who was determined to elevate and modernize the clerical education of his faith so that it might survive the intense competition from Roman Catholicism then sponsored by the Polish government.

[11] Kovalinskii, "Zhizn' Grigoriia Skovorody," p. 489; Stelletskii, "Stranstvuiushchii ukrainskii filosof," pp. 451–542. Elizabeth reigned 1741–1762.

[12] Edie, *Russian Philosophy*, I, 11.

[13] For an excellent discussion of Plato's influence upon Skovoroda, see F. A. Zelenogorskii, "Filosofiia Grigoriia Savvicha Skovorody, ukrainskago filosofa xviii stoletiia" [Philosophy of Grigorii Savvich Skovoroda, Ukrainian philosopher of the eighteenth century], *Voprosy filosofii i psikhologii* [Questions of philosophy and psychology] 23 (1894): 222–227.

[14] This question is analyzed by Ern, *Grigorii Savvich Skovoroda*, p. 62, and Kovalinskii, "Zhizn' Grigoriia Skovorody," p. 502.

Roman writers[15] and the works of Philo the Jew.[16] Skovoroda
also acquired a fine knowledge of the early Church Fathers and
theologians,[17] both Eastern and Western, the latter indicating that
the study of Western thought in the Academy was not in vain.[18]
Skovoroda finally ended his studies in 1750, after showing himself to be the outstanding student in his class.[19] At the end, however, he must have disappointed both his teachers and his parents;
knowing that they hoped he would become a priest, but himself
lacking feeling for such an occupation, Grigorii suddenly began
to stutter in an extravagant, falsified voice.[20] A sly trick which

[15] Kovalinskii, "Zhizn' Grigoriia Skovorody," pp. 501, 502; Ern, *Grigorii Savvich Skovoroda*, p. 62; Zelenogorskii, "Filosofiia Skovorody,"
pp. 200–201; Skovoroda, *Tvori*, II, 159–189.

[16] Zelenogorskii, "Filosofiia Skovorody," pp. 230–234, presents an extended and specific analysis of Philo the Jew's influence on Skovoroda.

[17] Gustav Shpet, *Ocherk razvitiia russkoi filosofii* [Study of the development of Russian philosophy] (Petrograd, 1922), pp. 70, 74, denies
that Skovoroda was a highly educated person. Shpet concedes that Skovoroda had some knowledge of ancient philosophy and the Church
Fathers, but doubts a firsthand acquaintance with Plato, certainly not
enough to justify calling Skovoroda a Russian successor to Plato, as
many historians have done. E. Radlov is friendlier to Skovoroda as a
person, but in his *Ocherk istorii russkoi filosofii* [Study of the history
of Russian philosophy] (Peterburg [*sic*], 1920), p. 10, Radlov, too,
fails to find in Skovoroda great scholarship. From my own study of
Skovoroda's works, I think Shpet and Radlov greatly underestimate
Skovoroda's learning.

[18] Zenkovsky, *History of Russian Philosophy*, I, 53. Some of Skovoroda's education, however, may have been the result of an independent
approach. Ern suggests (*Grigorii Savvich Skovoroda*, p. 64), for example, that Origen's method of biblical interpretation made him suspect
with the Russian church hierarchy, although Skovoroda took his approach from Origen and made it a basic feature of his own thought.

[19] Ern, *Grigorii Savvich Skovoroda*, p. 51.

[20] This is the account of Skovoroda's personal friend, Gustav Gess-

produced its desired result! Skovoroda was excluded from the Academy and permitted to lay his own plans for the future.

Skovoroda was now twenty-eight years old and anxious to find new fields of learning which he did not and could not have in his native land.[21] He happily joined in that very year a diplomatic mission sent to improve relations with the Orthodox Church of Hungary.[22] Evidently Skovoroda succeeded in gaining permission to detach himself from his Russian colleagues, for during almost three years he toured Hungary, Poland, Austria, and much of Germany on foot.[23] He attended lectures at several universities and viewed many of the cultural monuments in Central Europe. Although it is most unlikely that Skovoroda was positively influenced then (or later) by contact with contemporary European thought,[24] he did return to Russia in 1753 with a splendid knowledge of German[25] and a broad and enduring respect for foreign peoples and their civilizations.

---

de-Kal've, writing in *Ukrainskii Vestnik* [Ukrainian Herald] in 1817, as cited in ibid., p. 49.

[21] Kovalinskii, "Zhizn' Grigoriia Skovorody," p. 489.

[22] Skovoroda might have served as interpreter, or as one knowledgeable in the Eastern service and music. See ibid., p. 489.

[23] Some sources include Italy in Skovoroda's itinerary, but this is not confirmed by Kovalinskii, "Zhizn' Grigoriia Skovorody," pp. 489–490; see also Ern, *Grigorii Savvich Skovoroda*, pp. 54–59.

[24] I maintain this despite the contrary opinions of Arkhimandrit [Father Superior] Gavriil, *Istoriia filosofii* [History of philosophy], 6 vols. (Kazan, 1839–1840), VI, 54; and Stelletskii, "Stranstvuiushchii ukrainskii filosof," pp. 453–454. I am supported by Ern, *Grigorii Savvich Skovoroda*, pp. 63–64; and D. I. Bagalei (ed.), *Sochineniia Grigoriia Savvicha Skovorody* [Works of Grigorii Savvich Skovoroda], 2 vols. (Kharkov, 1894), I, xlviii–xlix.

[25] Kovalinskii, "Zhizn' Grigoriia Skovorody," pp. 489–490; Ern, *Gri-*

After his foreign travels, Skovoroda accepted an offer of a teaching position extended by Bishop Nikodim Strebnitskii at Pereiaslav Seminary in the Ukraine. Skovoroda experienced difficulties with the prevailing Church approach in matters of art and culture. Specifically, he attempted to reconstruct the teaching of poetics on the basis of the tonic system of Lomonosov, rejecting the traditional syllabic versification of Simeon Polotskii, which Skovoroda considered alien to the living realities of the Russian language. Being an independent and original educator, Skovoroda was determined to approach old problems in a new way; however, he showed no tact in dealing with Strebnitskii's successor, Bishop Ioann Kozlovich, and was dismissed from his post within a year.[26] He then served on two separate occasions as tutor to the son of an eminent noble family of the Ukraine,[27] traveled to the Troitse-Sergiev monastery, returned, homesick, to the Ukraine, where for a time he simply wandered. Finally, in the midst of an intense spiritual crisis, Skovoroda began to teach poetics, ancient

---

gorii Savvich Skovoroda, pp. 59–61, 63. Skovoroda's familiarity with Polish probably dated from earlier years. Khidzheu, "Grigorii Skovoroda," pp. 160–161; Zenkovsky, History of Russian Philosophy, I, 54–55.

[26] Ern, Grigorii Savvich Skovoroda, pp. 67–70; Stelletskii, "Stranstvuiushchii ukrainskii filosof," pp. 454–455; A. S. Lebedev, "G. S. Skovoroda kak bogoslov" [G. S. Skovoroda as a theologian], Voprosy filosofii i psikhologii 27 (1898): 176; I. A. Tabachnikov, writing in V. E. Evgrafov et al., Istoriia filosofii v SSSR [History of philosophy in the USSR], 5 vols. (Moscow, 1968–   ), I, 399–400. Kovalinskii idealizes the episode, calling it Skovoroda's "first exercise in firmness of spirit" ("Zhizn' Grigoriia Skovorody," p. 490).

[27] Concerning Skovoroda's sojourn in the home of Stefan Tamara, see Kovalinskii, "Zhizn' Grigoriia Skovorody," pp. 491–492, 496; Skovoroda, Tvori, II, 543; Ern, Grigorii Savvich Skovoroda, pp. 70–73, 93, 103.

languages, and Christian morals at Kharkov collegium, in the Ukraine.

The difficulties Skovoroda experienced at Kharkov exceeded even those suffered earlier at Pereiaslav. In the latter instance the orthodoxy of his faith was apparently not the point of conflict; but now, in response to tremendous internal pressures of the soul, Skovoroda began to develop a highly personal religious philosophy which alienated the less imaginative teachers of Kharkov collegium. Some of Grigorii's colleagues went so far as to incite students against him, forbidding the boys to converse or even be seen with him! Not that Skovoroda did not have support as well as opposition at Kharkov, notably from his employer, Ioasaf Mitkevich, the presiding bishop at Belgorod, a scholarly and reflective person whom Skovoroda later described as "an image of Christ, quiet, meek, and merciful, a pure mirror of virtue."[28] But even Skovoroda's relationship with Mitkevich illustrates the philosopher's stormy personality and growing need to follow a unique, individual course of action. At one point, Mitkevich suggested through a mutual friend that Grigorii Savvich become a monk so that he might be quickly promoted to the higher clergy. Skovoroda scornfully rejected the suggestion that he become a pharisee and enjoy the sweet and easy life of a monk.[29] In fact, by this time, Skovoroda actually wanted to leave Kharkov and was restrained only through Mitkevich's appeals to duty, and by an affection growing between Mikhail Ivanovich Kovalinskii, one

[28] Skovoroda, *Tvori*, II, 49–50. On Mitkevich, see Nadejda Gorodetzky, *Saint Tikhon Zadonsky, Inspirer of Dostoevsky* (London, 1951), p. 16.

[29] Kovalinskii, "Zhizn' Grigoriia Skovorody," p. 498; Lebedev, "G. S. Skovoroda kak bogoslov," p. 176.

of his students, and himself. By 1766, however, Porfirii Kraiskii had become bishop of Belgorod, and he, finding Skovoroda's ideas insupportable,[30] forced Skovoroda to leave the Kharkov collegium.

At this point, Skovoroda was forty-four years of age and without money, position, or good prospects for a worldly future. Not that the last mattered much, for in the wake of his disappointment after the Kharkov episode, Skovoroda never again sought employment under Church auspices. Rather, he spent the remaining twenty-eight years of his life (until his death in 1794) on the road, as a member of that wandering fraternity of mystics and "fools in Christ" which then figured so prominently in the spiritual life of Russia and the Ukraine. Kovalinskii tells us that during this period Skovoroda believed himself to be *alone*, and dug deeply into his internal self for wisdom. He saw in happiness, disappointment; in friends, betrayal; in attire, deception; in success, emptiness. So Grigorii Savvich sought the entirety of lightness and darkness without friends, happiness, guidance, or counsel.[31] It is perhaps in this part of his experience that the reader will find some of Skovoroda's most touching moments, his urgent presentiment that "the entire world sleeps,"[32] concealing within itself (as, in fact, did he) a hidden life of sadness and tears. In a poem he says,

> O lovely world! You are an ocean, a chasm,
> You are darkness, whirlwind, yearning, sorrow. . . .

[30] Lebedev, "G. S. Skovoroda kak bogoslov," p. 176; Ern, *Grigorii Savvich Skovoroda*, pp. 133–134; Stelletskii, "Stranstvuiushchii ukrainskii filosof," pp. 616–617; Zenkovsky, *History of Russian Philosophy*, I, 30–31.

[31] Kovalinskii, "Zhizn' Grigoriia Skovorody," p. 523.

[32] Skovoroda, *Tvori*, I, 3.

And elsewhere,

> This world has a splendid look,
> But within it lies the unsleeping worm.
> Woe unto you, world! You show me laughter,
> But within your soul you week in secret.[33]

And yet we need in no sense pity Skovoroda, for without doubt he was following the course he thought ordained for him, and in this he was happy. He lived poorly, without money, possessing only the clothes on his back. But it was Grigorii himself who once observed: "A good person will find his daily bread from people everywhere, and the earth will give him water free. More is not necessary!" Skovoroda punctuated his travels with visits to friends old and new among the nobility and peasantry of the Ukraine. While traveling, he made it his personal objective to live in harmony with nature and to practice various asceticisms— although none so harsh as to deny himself wine and brandy, or to suffocate himself in "pedantry and dry rigor." During the spring he slept under the stars, in gardens or beneath bushes; during the winter, in stables. The rest and contemplation he found on such occasions made night a moving experience for Skovoroda, a veritable refuge from the exertions and trials of the day. Many of Skovoroda's letters to Kovalinskii were written "at night."[34] In the quietness of a deep silence of feeling and nature, his thoughts turned easily to God.[35]

---

[33] From Zenkovsky, *History of Russian Philosophy*, I, 59, with slight revisions.

[34] See Edie, *Russian Philosophy*, I, 62, and, in general, Skovoroda's seventy-nine letters to Kovalinskii, reprinted in Skovoroda, *Tvori*, II, 211–390.

[35] Kovalinskii, "Zhizn' Grigoriia Skovorody," pp. 521–522.

A casual observer might have judged Skovoroda wretched and poor, but Grigorii fiercely resisted all efforts of others to change his pattern of life, although at various times friends implored him to join them as a monk,[36] Catherine the Great invited him to settle in the intellectual milieu of St. Petersburg,[37] and one admiring peasant father urged him to marry his kind and loving daughter. (At the very altar, Skovoroda finally made a hasty retreat.)[38] Perhaps Grigorii Skovoroda even sensed in friends a threat to his restless independence, for though he loved to visit, and the spiritual counsel he gave made him a most welcome guest, we know that sometimes he left his hosts suddenly, without warning.[39]

These were years of intense artistic and intellectual creativity for Skovoroda as he infused his feelings and ideas into a growing body of dialogs, letters, poems, songs, and fables—and even several Russian translations of ancient treatises on ethics and philosophy.[40] Perhaps it was in this period that Skovoroda resolved

[36] Ibid., pp. 509–510, 516.

[37] Skovoroda replied to the emissary bearing this proposal: "Tell our little mother [*matushka*, a most proper term for a Russian subject to use in referring to a lady ruler], the tsarina, that I will not abandon my homeland [the Ukraine]. My reed pipe and sheep are dearer to me than a sovereign's crown." Later, in 1787, while traveling through the Ukraine, Catherine visited Skovoroda and spoke with him. See Stelletskii, "Stranstvuiushchii ukrainskii filosof," pp. 612, 623.

[38] Ern, *Grigorii Savvich Skovoroda*, pp. 156–158.

[39] Zenkovsky, *History of Russian Philosophy*, I, 56.

[40] The discussion of Skovoroda's thought contained in this essay is based upon his dialogs (*Tvori*, vol. 1), and Kovalinskii's "Life of Grigorii Skovoroda" (*Tvori*, II, 487–535). Except for a few passages in Edie, *Russian Philosophy*, I, 58–62, most of his letters are available only in the original Latin or Greek with Ukrainian (!) translation in "Skovoroda" (*Tvori*, vol. II). Space limitations forbid discussion of

to be a "Russian Socrates," "one who will teach us first of all to know ourselves, so that . . . we may then develop out of ourselves a philosophy which will be our own, native and natural to our land . . ."[41] If Skovoroda did have such messianic aspirations, they, too, must be seen as an integral part of his life and values: "When my mind and heart will dwell in the house which wisdom created for itself in holy Russia, and I become drunk from the riches of that house, I will be as blessed as he who had his family in Zion. For in the mountains of Russia, I see everything new: new people, new animals, a new creation, and a new glory. Oh, how then will all be easy, merry, pleasant, loving and free! My thought flies through infinity, to the heights, to the depths, to the expanse—unhindered by mountains, seas, steppes."[42]

Skovoroda's Russian translations of Greek and Roman treatises, as well as his "creative literature" (see *Tvori*, vol. II).

[41] Quoted in Edie, *Russian Philosophy*, I, 17, as something Skovoroda might have said.

[42] The "Socrates passage" was included in the uncritical edition of Skovoroda's works published in St. Petersburg in 1861, but omitted in the later critical editions of 1894, 1912, and 1961 (see "Bibliographical Essay" below). An excellent discussion of its dubious authenticity (clearly the reason for its exclusion from the last three editions) is provided by Bagalei, *Sochineniia Skovorody*, I, xxiv, xxxi–xxxiv, lxvii–lxx. Since some passages are in Latin, I would suppose the document was produced by one of Skovoroda's educated friends, based upon a conversation with the master. As such, it probably reflects thoughts authentic with Skovoroda, but of this we can never be certain.

The longer passage which I have quoted from this "Socrates" document (not rendered by Edie in *Russian Philosophy*; see footnote 41 above), is from the 1861 *Sochineniia v stikhakh i proze Grigoriia Savicha* [sic] *Skovorody* [Works in poems and prose of Grigorii Savvich Skovoroda], p. 290. The document continues, growing steadily more ecstatic.

What, then, was this philosophy, capable of moving Skovoroda to such hope and ecstasy?

Skovoroda analyzed reality in terms of three interrelated "worlds": first, the natural world surrounding man, the macrocosm, the general world, wherein "everything which is born lives" —a realm which Skovoroda maintained is "comprised of an infinite world of worlds and is the great world"; second, the microcosm, the private "little world" of the human individual;[43] and third, the symbolical world of the Bible.[44] These worlds are interconnected. For example, the Bible "contains figures from creation which are heavenly, earthly, and infernal, designed to serve as monuments to lead our thought to an understanding of the eternal nature hidden within perishable [exterior reality] as a painting [is hidden] within its colors."[45] As for the macrocosm, it is relevant to the microcosm, and not simply in the evident sense of providing man his home.[46] Kovalinskii quotes Skovoroda as saying, "I believe and know that all which exists in the great world exists in the little world, too, and that whatever is possible in the small world is also possible in the great through their conformity to the unity of the all-pervading spirit."[47]

[43] Skovoroda uses the diminutive form of *mir* (world), *"myrik"* and *"mirok"*; see *Tvori*, I, p. 536.

[44] Skovoroda in his last dialog (1790), "Potop zmiin," [Flood of snakes], *Tvori*, I, especially p. 536. This analysis does not contradict his earlier ideas, however.

[45] Ibid., p. 536.

[46] Skovoroda also calls the macrocosm the "inhabited world" (*obitel'nyi mir*), ibid., p. 536.

[47] Kovalinskii, "Zhizn' Grigoriia Skovorody," p. 526.

For Skovoroda, all three worlds are dualistic, comprised as each is by both matter and spirit. For example, in the symbolical world, the Bible, we encounter an external layer of stories and episodes which are no more probable than a "flood of snakes" and therefore not meant actually to affect our ideas about the real world, the macrocosm.[48] In fact, this aspect of the Bible is a "divine tumult," a welter of shameless "lies."[49] But these "lies" possess great allegorical truth: "the lies will instruct us . . . because in the lies are imprinted tracks and pathways useful in leading the mind to an excellent truth."[50] Likewise Skovoroda asserts that each person has a human body which is visible and material and a mind which pervades the body and is unseen.[51] The great, macrocosmic world also discloses two natures: the objects of creation and God, who penetrates and fills all things.[52] Skovoroda sometimes compares this "celestial spirit" to the clever machinery which keeps a tower clock in operation.[53] In other cases he sees it as similar to the design concealed within the painting of a work of art,[54] yet elsewhere it is likened to the Platonic, archetypal

[48] The Bible "in no way affects the inhabited world, but only leads us with tracks gathered from creation to that sole, true reality, like a magnetic arrow gazing at its eternal solidity" (Skovoroda, *Tvori*, I, 384–385).

[49] Skovoroda tells us that if we are to understand the Bible literally, we must conclude that "in many places, shamelessly and badly, with no taste, it lies" (ibid., p. 551).

[50] Ibid., p. 375; see also p. 39.

[51] Ibid., pp. 16, 33–34.

[52] Ibid., p. 57.

[53] Ibid., pp. 16–17.

[54] Ibid., pp. 38, 536.

"idea,"[55] primary and uncreated, eternal and immaterial, yet casting a shadow which we perceive as the material thing.[56]

It is precisely the dualistic nature of reality which opens to man the greatest opportunities and dangers in the ordering and conduct of his life. Essentially Skovoroda tells us that the more we are involved in the external, material dimensions of our "three worlds," the less likely are we to attain the happiness that comes from knowledge of the essential and true. In one of his earliest dialogs,[57] Skovoroda speaks of Narcissus as one who made the fatal mistake of seeing in his bodily self the source of all beauty and meaning, and, taking self-knowledge to be nothing more than the comprehension of his body, he falls in love with his own image.[58] To Skovoroda this is *idol-worship*, a term he also uses to describe other states of mind. Some idol-worshippers may not be egotistical, they may even think they believe in one God; but these people really believe only in the crude elements before their eyes—and not in that which cannot be seen but only understood.[59] Similarly the "irrational" Christian zealot fails to see that whatever virtues church ceremonies might possess, they are at best a "weak shadow" of that real truth which is to be found only in God.[60] As for the "superstitious Christian," he insists on believing that Enoch and Ilias really flew through the heavens, that Navin stopped the sun, that the Jordan once backed up on its

[55] Skovoroda uses the words *videniia, vidy, obrazy* (ibid., pp. 48, 539).

[56] Ibid., pp. 33–37, 539.

[57] "Narkiss, razglagol o tom: znai sebe" [Narcissus, a discussion concerning self-knowledge], in ibid., pp. 27–82.

[58] Ibid., pp. 27–29, 32–33.

[59] Ibid., pp. 35–37, 256.

[60] Ibid., pp. 115–116, 123–124, 200.

course, that Mary was truly a virgin.[61] So fiercely did Skovoroda disdain this type of thought that at one point he says he finds atheism less objectionable than superstition, just as he would prefer the assertion that Plutarch never existed to a falsification of Plutarch's character.[62] Not that Skovoroda had real admiration for the atheist![63] Atheism, like idol-worship, represents nothing more than an inability to see beyond literal, material reality into that metaphysical realm which is the ontological ground of creation.

The wise man, for Skovoroda, is one who devotes himself to transcending the physical dimensions of the worlds in which we live. Most people, of course, are not wise, for they confuse happiness with the acquisition of things. They think that to be content they must live in a certain country, share high honor and rank, or be, as one character says in "A Conversation among Five Trav-

---

[61] Ibid., p. 270. Some of these episodes appear to be from the Russian Apocrypha.

[62] Skovoroda notes that not only does the superstitious man attack the laws of nature, he brands those who disagree with him "heretics." Superstitious people use the Bible, but in the literal approach they fail to grasp the higher sense contained within its allegories and figures of speech (Ibid., pp. 375, 383, 386–388).

[63] The story is told of a learned atheist who chided Skovoroda: "It's a shame that you, having studied so well, live like a crazy person, without a goal or any use for society." To which Grigorii Savvich replied: "You are right! Until now I have done nothing useful—but, I must say, nothing harmful, either. But you, sir, with your Godlessness alone have already done much evil: a person without faith is a hellish beast in nature. Our conscience is easy when we have harmed no one, if fate has put us in a place in which we are unable to display greater usefulness" (Gess-de-Kal've in *Ukrainskii Vestnik* 6 [1817]; 115–116, as cited in Zelenogorskii, "Filosofiia Skovorody," p. 207 n.; see also p. 217 concerning Skovoroda's opinions on atheism).

ellers concerning Life's True Happiness," "as rich as a bull in furs."[64] In a similar vein, Farra, a participant in another dialog,[65] is excited by the report of a certain "prophet" in Europe who makes a juice from herbs which restores youth to him and his friends; the news of a physician who lived without sickness for three hundred years by eating only bread and water; and the story of an astrakhan sheep with eyes which could see farther and more clearly than a man with a telescope. Poor Farra! He tells us that *his* eyes get weaker day by day, and he fails to see how he will manage to live another twenty years! "Who and which land," he asks, "will restore youth to me? My term is coming to an end!"

In closely reasoned terms, Skovoroda attempts to answer this materialistic sentiment. He asks: What is happiness? Is it something we experience by living at a certain time (*e.g.*, in the age of Solomon)? In a certain place (America, the Canary Islands, on a desert, or in royal palaces)? Does happiness come from riches, station, education, or health? If so, Skovoroda sagely observes, most men would be poor.[66] For many do not have these things; and some who do are ruined by them. So the thing in and of itself does not bring about that state of mind men know as "happiness"—if for no reason other than the simple fact that things material are transient, while the feeling after which we search must be an eternal, indelible part of our experience.[67]

---

[64] Edie, *Russian Philosophy*, I, 27.

[65] "Beseda, narechennaia dvoe, o tom, chto blazhennym byt' legko" [A Discussion of (life's) two principles (material and spiritual): (showing) that it is easy to be good], in Skovoroda, *Tvori*, I, 162–186.

[66] Ibid., pp. 14–15.

[67] Ibid., p. 307.

Thus one of Farra's friends answers him in these words: "One person dies at thirty, another at three hundred. If dying is a misfortune, then both are poor. A prisoner's comfort is small if they take others to the gallows in three hours and him in thirty days. What is health, even, to me, if weakness comes at the end? What is youth when it gives way to old age? Ah, don't call something sweet if it brings about misfortune. Don't make something durable which comes to an end. Don't make happiness something which will come to an end. Judge every affair from its fruit and from its end."[68]

Skovoroda does not mean to say that one cannot be happy if one is rich, learned, and healthy. He merely insists that if one is happy in any of those circumstances it is not the situation itself which produces happiness. For happiness is something all men need and desire, and *Nature*—which is ever kind and bountiful— holds its possibility open to everyone, even to those who are old or sick or poor or not (formally) educated. One might be happy as a soldier or a farmer,[69] even as a miser fearful over the loss of his hoard.[70] But since we also find unhappy people here, an army career, farming, and miserliness clearly are not themselves the effective cause of happiness, not even to those soldiers, farmers, and misers who *are* happy. Likewise, since these callings are closed to most, they in no sense represent the necessary, *universal* road to happiness. That path is found only by transcending the

---

[68] Ibid., pp. 163–164.

[69] Ibid., pp. 348–352.

[70] See Edie, *Russian Philosophy*, I, 58. I do not think, incidentally, that Skovoroda actually believed one might be happy pursuing the life of a miser, certainly not in comparison with the man who philosophizes "in Christ."

objects and estates of material reality, by asking: What are the things in life we *really* need? Which elements are absolutely necessary to our well-being, representing not superfluous things of idle concern, but articles indispensable to our genuine welfare? Skovoroda concedes that we must have such things as air and sunshine, water and bread.[71] Perhaps without these basic things we could not be happy—but the search for more than this leads toward greed, restlessness, dishonesty. A life devoted to materialistic qualities cannot be a life of spiritual thirst and satisfaction; such a life cannot be peaceful and contented. Skovoroda's reflections concerning the things men truly need in order to be happy provide one of his most arresting observations: the paradox that it is easy to obtain the things we need, but so very difficult—if not impossible—to attain the things we do *not* need![72]

Each man needs to find the kingdom of God, which in Skovoroda's allegorical terms might be understood as the internal peace, order, and joy which we feel by loving God, comprehending His divine order, and reveling in the glory of His wisdom as contained in the Scriptures. Because the divine spirit pervades all three worlds, experience in one inevitably leads to its equivalent in others: the Bible instructs one equally in the glory of the cosmos and the nature of the soul . . . and to know oneself is to know God . . . just as insight into Moses is the same as insight into Jesus. Actually, the kingdom of God is already within each person.[73] To find it, Skovoroda believes, one need but ask in the

[71] Ibid., pp. 54–55. Skovoroda, *Tvori*, I, 27–29, 179.

[72] Skovoroda, *Tvori*, pp. 14, 29, 162–186, 459. See also Kovalinskii, "Zhizn' Grigoriia Skovorody," pp. 521, 525.

[73] Skovoroda, *Tvori*, I, 103, 253.

name of Christ,[74] which means to learn to philosophize in Christ.[75] Attaining this kingdom makes one see that happiness does not come through possessions or worldly circumstances but only through living poorly and humbly, in conformity with the "secret law" of Nature and God, resisting that hunger for riches and honors that leads one so easily from the true path. Man needs only a truth which is eternal, spiritual, and whole.[76]

But most people do not find the kingdom of heaven. God gives to each the freedom to choose one path or the other,[77] yet most incline toward the fleshly, satanic element of their being, which bears fruit after its own kind as surely as does the spiritual, angelic element. They listen to the "devil," whom Skovoroda describes as a slanderer and calumniator using machinations to steer one from the good to an evil path leading to the kingdom of darkness. Unable to believe in the existence of the unseen, most people seek pleasure, life, strength, and beauty in *things*. They love what they see and weep for it when it is gone, like a baby who sobs over a smashed nut, not understanding that the "true nut essence" rests not in the shell, but in the seed "within the innermost shell, upon which the very crust depends." Truly, says Skovoroda, these people have ignored God and harkened to the sirens, "sweet-talking fool[s] leading you to build your happiness upon that rock which will not endure, but will break."[78]

Skovoroda displayed a consistent interest in the reality of death,

[74] Ibid., pp. 179, 181.
[75] Ibid., p. 200.
[76] Ibid., p. 307.
[77] Ibid., pp. 482–485.
[78] Ibid., pp. 48, 165.

interpreting it as a wall which separates light from darkness, the familiar from the unknown. At times his concern reveals an anxious quality, as when he asks: Why does life end in death? How is it possible that flesh and blood are fated to become mere dust and ashes? Is death—and not life—alone and everywhere triumphant?[79] On this particular occasion, Skovoroda consoled himself with the idea that the true man never dies; his arms, legs, body decay, and "return" to the soil. But he, a true servant of God, remains with his master forever.[80] Does Skovoroda believe, then, literally, in heaven and hell? What of the idea of resurrection? In these areas, frankly, I find his thinking unclear. Probably he quietly rejected literal notions of paradise and hell, anticipating simply a mystical union between God and the genuine believer —expressing no real opinion concerning the fate of the remainder. As for resurrection, just as Paul raised the bodies of the dead, and Jesus is now among the eternally living,[81] so, too, the Lord "carries us from the mountain to the valley, [and] delivers us again to that very same mountain."[82] Little wonder that Skovoroda, bound by such convictions, characteristically overcame fear of death, seeing it simply as the logical fate of the external, dustlike shell of the internal spirit. He found absurd the ancient Egyptians' practice of mummification, or their hope of discovering a potion to extend life for thousands of years.[83] Skovoroda poses an interesting question: If a child in the womb could think,

[79] For example, in "Narcissus," written just before 1767, when Skovoroda was forty-five years old. Ibid., pp. 69–70.

[80] Ibid., pp. 71–72.

[81] Ibid., pp. 69, 200.

[82] Ibid., p. 68; see also pp. 276 and 277–296 passim.

[83] Kovalinskii, "Zhizn' Grigoriia Skovorody," p. 525.

would he see that birth opens up a new, better life of freedom and light? "In the same manner does life after death seem impossible to those imprisoned in this transient life."[84]

In the final analysis, of course, Skovoroda regarded death as a mystery, a phenomenon we experience, but fail truly to comprehend. Skovoroda expressed a similar view of the existence of evil—although here, I suspect, he failed to account for its reality in terms entirely satisfactory even to himself. If I am correct in my understanding of this question, Skovoroda, despite his irascible and intransigent character, was a person of profound, fundamental goodness, one who experienced life as a poetic encounter with beauty, truth, and love. As such, I suspect he was unable to grasp fully the presence in life of blind forces arbitrarily working upon men: tragedy and woe. Often, in fact, his philosophizing seems to ignore evil, and, in the final analysis, his explanation of it lacks profundity—although not necessarily conviction. In an early dialog[85] one speaker tells us, "evil people have lost their hearts (i.e., themselves)," which is to say that evil is the final fruit of a failure in man to seek the transcendent good. Interestingly enough, no one in the dialog is satisfied with this account; their discussion of the question ends, uneasily, with the idea that perhaps man's range and depth of comprehension is so small that he is simply unable to see the logic behind the presence of evil in life. To this Skovoroda adds the suggestion that God "divided all things in two for you, so that you would not confuse darkness with light, falsehood with truth."[86] "Who could speak

---

[84] Ibid., p. 51.
[85] "Narcissus," in Skovoroda, Tvori, I, 50–51.
[86] Ibid., p. 51.

of whiteness without a knowledge of blackness? Taste alone detects the bitter and sweet."[87]

Students of Grigorii Skovoroda's life and thought have characteristically concluded—as did I, at one point—that Skovoroda felt himself to be intellectually estranged from the Russian Orthodox Church. I. A. Tabachnikov interprets Skovoroda's difficulties at Kharkov collegium as stemming from "a critical stance toward the Bible and religion with [which] the prevailing views of churchmen collided."[88] Vladimir Ern believes that Skovoroda, although "not in principle disaffected from the Church, nevertheless stood in a certain mute, unconscious opposition to it."[89] Even such a church scholar as V. V. Zenkovsky is convinced that Skovoroda "stood in opposition to traditional ecclesiastical doctrines."[90]

It is true that Skovoroda had difficulties with the Church, although these were usually the result of his own tactless, restive, uncompromising personality. Skovoroda was a man who thought freely, and he prized highly the lack of occupation and commitments which permitted him to roam at will throughout southern

[87] Ibid., p. 62; in later dialogs see pp. 136, 343.

[88] Evgrafov, *Istoriia filosofii v SSSR*, I, 400.

[89] Ern, *Grigorii Savvich Skovoroda*, p. 325.

[90] Although Zenkovsky complicates his argument by stating (elsewhere) that Skovoroda represented a current of opinion which related "without hostility or suspicion toward the Church" (*History of Russian Philosophy*, I, 53, 57), oddly enough, I think Zenkovsky here, too, is wrong. I would characterize Skovoroda as *suspicious* of the Church and *hostile* to certain of its features; but I do not find in Skovoroda "opposition to traditional ecclesiastical doctrines."

Russia and the Ukraine. Doubtless some churchmen thought him heretical[91]—although others (as we have seen) esteemed him and sought his cooperation. Skovoroda clearly had an original mind and a contentious spirit. But was he at odds, as a thinker or a communicant, with the organized Russian Church?

On balance, I think not, and I justify my view by asking of established opinion: "In what respect, precisely, was Skovoroda organically disaffected from the Church? Zenkovsky thinks that Skovoroda's allegorical method of understanding the Bible carried him well beyond the confines of established Church thought,[92] while Ern suggests that some of the early theologians of interest to Skovoroda were in dubious standing with the Russian Church.[93] Without denying *elements* of truth in these conclusions, I think we must not exaggerate their total significance. For example, Ern himself notes that the allegorical method of biblical interpretation was by no means unprecedented in Russia: it flourished for centuries in the Alexandria school and passed through Maximus the Confessor, John of Damascus, and others to become an element in Eastern Orthodoxy's comprehension of the Bible.[94] Surely, Skovoroda was more of an "allegorist" than

[91] See Edie, *Russian Philosophy*, I, 21–22.

[92] Zenkovsky, *History of Russian Philosophy*, I, 53.

[93] Origen was "under suspicion and virtually considered a heretic," while Dionysius Areopagiticus and Maximus the Confessor, although "profoundly authoritative in antiquity . . . were not at all popular with the ordinary representatives of Eastern Orthodoxy . . ." (Ern, *Grigorii Savvich Skovoroda*, p. 64).

[94] Whereby Origen scoffed at the idea of three days without the sun, or the story of Adam hiding from God, concluding: "Is it possible to doubt that all this may be understood only in a symbolical sense?" (Ibid., p. 242.)

the average, poorly educated cleric (who might have been totally a "literalist"). But let us not overestimate the extent to which Skovoroda himself rejected the letter of Scripture in favor of higher, symbolical meaning! If he ridicules the credulity required to believe that the sun stopped or the Jordan backed up in its course,[95] elsewhere in his works he has no doubt that St. Paul really raised the dead.[96] And if Skovoroda sees the Book of Exodus as a lesson in gaining self-knowledge, thinking that "it is clear that to leave Egypt means to escape from death to life,"[97] without doubt Skovoroda thought that the flight of Moses and the Jews was a genuine event in history.[98]

Skovoroda's interpretation of society as a dualistic complex of three interrelated "worlds" represents independent thinking— but no essential departure from the tenets of Eastern Orthodoxy. His views on heaven and hell are fairly bold; his approach to the problem of evil and death almost disappointingly conventional. During the early nineteenth century Church censors might remove passages of a published dialog suggesting that to "know" Moses is to know Christ,[99] but these vigilant readers apparently were untroubled by Skovoroda's other basic concepts. Least of all would Skovoroda's understanding of God give rise to disagreement. In some cases Skovoroda does speak of God as an imper-

[95] Skovoroda, *Tvori*, I, 270.
[96] Ibid., pp. 3, 69.
[97] Ibid., p. 140.
[98] Ibid., pp. 140–141.
[99] These deletions occurred in early pages of Skovoroda's dialog "Achsah," ibid., pp. 87–88. See Vladimir Bonch-Bruevich (ed.), *Sobranie Sochinenii G. S. Skovorody* [Collected works of G. S. Skovoroda], 2 vols. (St. Petersburg, 1912–   ) I, 128–129.

sonal *force* which "permeates and fills all of creation,"[100] giving it substance, design, and motion.[101] But he does not end with the Enlightenment idea of God as the "Great Watchmaker," for in other passages of his dialogs he conceives of God as a *being* vexed by human failings and speaks of faith in God provoking in him both fear and love of the Lord.[102] Nor does Skovoroda expound a heretical, pantheistic interpretation of God, despite the impression one might have after a first encounter with his ideas.[103] As a dualist, Skovoroda does maintain that God penetrates man and nature. In a tree, God is the true tree; in grass, the true grass; in music, the music; in a house, the house; in our body, the body.[104] But Skovoroda specifically says, in the latter instance, that the flesh *itself* is not God—nor God the flesh.[105] God is *in* everything, imparting to each thing its true, specific essence. But "this word 'true' also fixes *the most profound boundary* between empirical and noumenal, between external and internal. God is nature, but a *second* nature, created and uncreated, eternal, containing within itself a primary world, *i.e., a world in his* [God's] *eternal idea.* The unity of God with *this* world is not pantheism, . . .

[100] Skovoroda, *Tvori*, I, 57.

[101] Ibid., pp. 38, 42.

[102] Ibid., p. 63.

[103] This is actually the interpretation of I. A. Tabachnikov, who argues that Skovoroda's ideas before the mid-1770's were already semi-pantheistic, while in later years he moved totally toward the position that God *is* nature. Tabachnikov concludes: "These and other pantheistic formulations of Skovoroda are derived from the principle of Spinoza, 'Deus sive Natura' " (Evgrafov, *Istoriia filosofii v SSSR*, I, 403).

[104] Skovoroda, *Tvori*, I, 39–41.

[105] Ibid., p. 58.

[for] like Giordano Bruno, [Skovoroda] draws a metaphysical distinction between God and the world."[106]

Just as a careful study of Skovoroda's thought reveals its basic harmony with established Church teaching, so does a study of his life suggest a surprisingly close attachment to the institutional forms of the Russian Church. (Although, again, Skovoroda displays independence, even willfulness!) For example, if Skovoroda sometimes criticized monasticism, he also admired some monastic figures of the past,[107] and did not seek to draw others from the monk's calling.[108] True, Grigorii Skovoroda seldom went to church, although once, in discussing the question with Bishop Tikhon III of Voronezh, Skovoroda told the prelate, "if it pleases you, I will go tomorrow," which he did.[109] On another occasion, at mass, he approached the priest to receive Communion. The priest, knowing Skovoroda's "strangeness," and fearing to communicate an impenitent, asked: "Do you know what a great sin you will consummate, not being prepared [for Communion]? And are you ready for this great mystery?" To which

---

[106] Ern, *Grigorii Savvich Skovoroda*, p. 262. Emphasis in the original.

[107] Pavel Fiveiskii, St. Anthony, or Savva Osviashchennyi; see Skovoroda, *Tvori*, I, 180, and Zelenogorskii, "Filosofiia Skovorody," p. 202.

[108] The monks of the *pecherskaia lavra* (near Kiev) begged Skovoroda to join them when he was visiting there in 1764. Skovoroda rejected the invitation in harsh terms. Later, one of the monks said to Skovoroda: "O wise man! I myself have had the same thought you related yesterday before our brotherhood, but I was never able to find my thoughts. I feel I was not born to this black attire, and having taken it up from a kind of piety, I torment myself. Am I able to [follow the monk's calling]?" Skovoroda answered, "With man it is impossible, but from God all things are possible" (Kovalinskii, "Zhizn' Grigoriia Skovorody," pp. 509–510).

[109] Stelletskii, "Stranstvuiushchii ukrainskii filosof," p. 622.

Skovoroda replied that he knew and was ready—and took the Eucharist.[110] From this episode, we conclude that Skovoroda was no more willing to cut himself off from the organized body of the faithful than he was able to accept what seemed to him to be "superstitious" elements of Church dogma (*e.g.*, the "danger" of taking Communion without first submitting to confession and penance). The story of Skovoroda's death urges us still more strongly to realize his basic attachment to the Church. At first, while failing, he resisted suggestions that he accept the last rites, saying such things were not needed for one "truly a believer." But then he relented, and before death received the Sacrament.[111]

Toward the very end of his life, Skovoroda met his friend, Mikhail Kovalinskii, in the Orlov region, in the Ukraine. Skovoroda was then seventy-two years old and must have had a presentiment of death. He entrusted all of his remaining manuscripts to Kovalinskii, and, parting from him on August 26, 1794, he said: "Perhaps I shall never see you again. Farewell! Always remember in all your adventures in life the things about which we so often spoke: light and dark, the head and the tail, good and evil, eternity and time. My spirit sees in you the highest ability to accept the truth and love it."[112] From Orlov, Skovoroda traveled yet a while, visiting friends he loved, ending, finally, in the village of Ivanovka (near Kursk), at the estate of the landowner Andrei Kovalevskii. In this place Skovoroda died peacefully on October 29, 1794. In response to his last request, Skovoroda's friends placed upon his tombstone an epitaph which captures marvel-

---

[110] Ibid., p. 622.
[111] Kovalinskii, "Zhizn' Grigoriia Skovorody," p. 531.
[112] Ibid., p. 530.

ously the essence of his life and soul: "The world hunted me, but it did not catch me."[113]

It would be inspiring to close this discussion of Skovoroda's life and thought with the suggestion that he had a great influence upon later generations. But the question of Skovoroda's influence is surprisingly complex, and apparently admits of no clear or easy solution. Although he published nothing during his lifetime (probably because of his wanderlust and extreme poverty),[114] Skovoroda was obviously concerned to commit his ideas to paper and put the manuscripts in reliable hands. These manuscripts and a considerable apocrypha based upon them were popular[115] and were broadly disseminated throughout southern Russia and the Ukraine[116] and reached as far as Bulgaria, Rumania, and Poland.[117] Many of the Ukrainian nobles who raised 400,000 rubles in 1802 to establish Kharkov University were among Skovoroda's

[113] Ibid., p. 531. See also Ern, *Grigorii Savvich Skovoroda*, pp. 203–205, and Stelletskii, "Stranstvuiushchii ukrainskii filosof," pp. 475–476.

[114] Bagalei's interpretation, *Sochineniia Skovorody*, I, i–ii. Bagalei also thinks it possible that Skovoroda wanted to keep his thoughts from "literary enemies," some of whom would have liked to harass or even jail him. Ern thinks it more likely that Skovoroda felt so involved with his ideas that he wanted to keep them from "unworthy hands" (Ern, *Grigorii Savvich Skovoroda*, pp. 170, 171–172, 175, 177). It is true that Skovoroda characteristically gave his manuscripts to Kovalinskii and other close friends.

[115] For example, the "Socrates in Russia" passage, or some interesting material in Bagalei, *Sochineniia Skovorody*, II, 309–344.

[116] Kovalinskii, "Zhizn' Grigoriia Skovorody," pp. 519, 529–530. Bagalei, *Sochineniia Skovorody*, I, i–ii.

[117] Evgrafov, *Istoriia filosofii v SSSR*, I, 400.

friends and admirers and were motivated by a desire to pay tribute to the philosopher's ability to excite in them love of knowledge.[118] Writing in 1835, some forty years after Skovoroda's death, Khidzheu notes that Skovoroda was still popular with the "simple people of the Ukraine"[119] who elevated him to the level of an archetypal hero and made his songs, parables, and sayings so popular that much was attributed to Grigorii Savvich that was not truly original with him.[120] As late as 1861 the Russian folklorist and historian Kostomarov noted of Skovoroda: "In the entire area from Ostrogozhsk to Kiev, his portrait hangs in many houses; every literate Ukrainian knows of him, as do many of the illiterate folk. His wayfaring life is the object of stories and anecdotes. In several places, descendants of fathers and uncles know of places he visited, in which he loved to abide—and point them out with pride. Skovoroda's good disposition to many contemporaries comprises the familial pride of their grandsons."[121]

The evidence justifies, perhaps, the conclusion that Skovoroda

[118] Bagalei, *Sochineniia Skovorody*, I, pp. xlii, xliv–xlv. Ern, *Grigorii Savvich Skovoroda*, p. 195. For a most precise and informative discussion of how Skovoroda helped to lay the intellectual foundations for the establishment of Kharkov University, see D. I. Bagalei, *Opyt istorii Khar'kovskago universiteta* [Attempt at a history of Kharkov University], 2 vols. (Kharkov, 1898), I, 25–33.

[119] *"prostoi narod Ukrainy"* (Khidzheu, "Grigorii Skovoroda," pp. 13–14).

[120] Kline has noted of Skovoroda: "Like Socrates and Confucius he is one of the truly legendary figures in the history of philosophy—whose life and oral teachings contained an enigma, a secret which even the most careful study of his writings does not reveal" (Edie, *Russian Philosophy*, I, 14).

[121] Cited by Ern, *Grigorii Savvich Skovoroda*, p. 195.

was effective as a teacher of the people. He influenced the folk-
lore and popular culture of the Ukraine.[122] He may have shaped
some features of Old Believer thought in the region;[123] perhaps
he even stimulated friends toward their own philosophizing within the original framework of his ideas.[124] But we must emphasize
that Skovoroda influenced neither the established pattern of
Church thought nor the new currents of secular or mystical opinion forming in Russia by the time of his death.[125] Paradoxically,
Russian mysticism and antirationalism of the late eighteenth century—and the romantic thought which followed in its wake during the early nineteenth century—stemmed from the activities of
Russian Freemasonry and the translated writings of such Western
mystics as Jacob Boehme, Heinrich Stilling, or Louis Claude de
Saint-Martin.[126] Since Skovoroda's writings were not published
in his own lifetime, he had no opportunity to speak to the urban,

---

[122] Stelletskii, "Stranstvuiushchii ukrainskii filosof," p. 608.

[123] See Shpet, *Ocherk*, p. 69. Also Paul Miliukov, *Ocherki po istorii
russkoi kul'tury* [Studies in the history of Russian culture], 4th ed., part
2: *Tserkov' i shkola* [Church and school] (St. Petersburg, 1905), pp.
113–118.

[124] Ern, *Grigorii Savvich Skovoroda*, p. 177.

[125] Radlov puts it succinctly: "Skovoroda did not have a great influence
on the development of philosophy; he left behind a circle of admirers,
but did not create a school" (*Ocherk*, p. 11).

[126] Nicholas V. Riasanovsky, *Russia and the West in the Teaching
of the Slavophiles* (Gloucester, Mass.: Peter Smith, 1965), pp. 12, 13.
Nicholas Berdiaev, *The Russian Idea* (Boston: Beacon Press, 1962),
p. 19. See also Zdenek V. David, "The Influence of Jacob Boehme on
Russian Religious Thought," *Slavic Review* 21 (March 1962): 43–64,
especially p. 49. David believes that Boehme's influence at the Kiev
Academy was considerable at the time Skovoroda was a student there,
and that Skovoroda ("the first significant philosopher produced in
Russia") was much indebted to Boehme and his Russian followers.

Westernized intellectual of Russia in the age of Catherine the Great. When his philosophical dialogs began to be published (individually) during the early nineteenth century, they may have impressed a few educated clerics of the period. But the first anthology of his work, published in 1861, encountered a negative reaction from the radical, materialistic critics who then dominated Russian intellectual life. To "progressive" thinkers of the period Skovoroda's ideas seemed "scholastic,"[127] commonplace, lacking in significance. Later, at the turn of the twentieth century, educated Russians came increasingly to abandon the dry, prosaic rationalism and revolutionary sentiment of earlier years, and, in their new appreciation for the old treasures of Russian spirituality, Skovoroda began to be studied and appreciated. From the first centennial of his death (1894) through the 1920's editions of his works were published, accompanied by at least a few books, articles, and essays on his life and teachings. He could scarcely have been appreciated in the Soviet Union during the harsh years of intellectual Stalinism beginning in the 1930's. But finally came the "thaw," and in 1961 the first publication of his complete works at Kiev. The influence which Skovoroda's ideas will exercise upon the young people of our generation is still unclear. But to all those who read his work with an honest heart and a clear mind, Skovoroda will provide a challenge not dissimilar to that of Tolstoy or Socrates. In fact, comparison of Skovoroda with Socrates is not excessive or unjustified, for as one student has noted:

Both Socrates and Skovoroda felt from above the calling to be tutors

---

[127] Ern, *Grigorii Savvich Skovoroda*, pp. 210–211; Bagalei, *Sochineniia Skovorody*, I, xxxiv–xxxvi.

of the people, and, accepting the calling, they became public teachers in the personal and elevated meaning of that word. A living sense of duty as the developed demand of conscience towards being . . . served Socrates as his daemon, and Skovoroda as the Raphael of his heart, the originator and sustainer of his new glory, which reconciled his actions and entire life with the high order of things. . . . According to the teaching of Skovoroda, as with Socrates, the fundamental origin and foundation of knowledge is self-understanding. Similar to Socrates, interpreting for the Greek people the text of human nature according to the palmistry of common-sense, Skovoroda explicated for simple Russian people the very same text, but with the revelation of celestial reason. And Skovoroda, also like Socrates, not being limited by time or place, taught on the crossroads, at markets, by a cemetery, under church porticoes, during holidays, when his sharp word would articulate an intoxicated will—and in the hard days of the harvest, when a rainless sweat poured upon the earth. Everywhere he found the idea: for he who truly has the idea and is guided by it from the heart, from the soul, that person encounters his idea everywhere.[128]

[128] Gavriil, *Istoriia filosofii*, VI, 60–61.

BIBLIOGRAPHICAL ESSAY

The following materials were of great value in the preparation of this essay. Items are arranged chronologically within each category. In the case of bibliographical rarities I have noted libraries possessing those books and journals, and express thanks to them for allowing me access to those titles.

EDITIONS OF SKOVORODA'S WORK

Sochineniia v stikakh i proze Grigoriia Savicha [*sic*] *Skovorody* [Works in poems and prose of Grigorii Savvich Skovoroda] (St. Petersburg, 1861) [Columbia University] is the earliest comprehensive edition of Skovoroda's writings. It is useful for several pages of Skovoroda apocrypha (although such material is not so identified), but lacks notes, commentaries, and bibliography, so that in comparison with the next three versions of Skovoroda's work this book has little more than curiosity value. Dmitrii Bagalei's *Sochineniia Grigoriia Savvicha Skovorody* [Works of Grigorii Savvich Skovoroda], 2 vols. (Kharkov, 1894) [Library of Congress] must be recommended for a 131-page "Introduction," which discusses, among other things, the history of the printing of Skovoroda's various works, the merits of source materials and studies concerning Skovoroda's life and thought, and comments upon many of his dialogs and pieces of "creative literature." Vladimir Bonch-Bruevich planned an extensive two-volume edition of Skovoroda's works, but only the first volume containing the dialogs appeared at St. Petersburg in 1912, entitled *Sobranie Sochinenii G. S. Skovorody* [Collected works of

G. S. Skovoroda] [University of Chicago]. Its unique features include extensive corrections of texts which were published earlier by Bagalei, notes referring to biblical passages which probably inspired Skovoroda's thought in numerous cases, and brief essays surveying critically the different manuscript versions of each work published in the volume.

The best edition of Skovoroda's writings is Grigorii Skovoroda, *Tvori v dvokh tomakh* [Works in two volumes] (Kiev, 1961), published under the editorship of O. I. Bilets'kii, I. A. Tabachnikov, and other Soviet scholars. Unfortunately its lengthy "Introduction" and notes (which include varia of published texts and exceed 100 pages), as well as translations of Skovoroda's many letters written in Latin and Greek, are given only in Ukrainian, which means that these volumes will do remarkably little to elevate Skovoroda to something higher than the status of a provincial Ukrainian thinker. For some reason this edition lacks bibliographical information. George L. Kline is to be congratulated for his fine English translation of the greater part of "A Conversation among Five Travellers concerning Life's True Happiness," contained in vol. I. James M. Edie et al., eds. and trans., *Russian Philosophy*, 3 vols. (Chicago: Quadrangle Books, 1965). Professor Edie translated a few passages from Skovoroda's letters for this same anthology.

SECONDARY WORKS ON SKOVORODA'S LIFE AND THOUGHT

I am familiar with books devoted to Skovoroda and his philosophy by Vladimir Ern, *Grigorii Savvich Skovoroda, zhizn' i uchenie* [Grigorii Savvich Skovoroda: life and teachings] (Moscow, 1912) [Columbia University], and Domet Oljančyn, *Hryhorij Skoworoda, 1722–1794; der ukrainische Philosoph des xviii. Jahrhunderts und seine geistig-kulturelle Umwelt* (Berlin, 1928) [Harvard]. Ern's work is valuable for an extensive and critical discussion of Skovoroda's philosophy, although sometimes he attributes to Skovoroda positions which reflect the author more than his subject. Oljančyn's presentation is systematic but not imaginative. Its bibliography is relatively up-to-date, which I understand is also the case with Dmitrii Chizhevskii's Skovoroda bibliography in *Der Russische Gedanke*, I (1929).

The earliest study of Skovoroda's life and teachings is Mikhail Ivanovich Kovalinskii's "Zhizn' Grigoriia Skovorody" [Life of Grigorii Skovoroda], written in 1796, two years after Skovoroda's death, and not published until 1886. It is nearly hagiographic in tone, yet contains numerous insights into the soul of its subject and expounds brilliantly many aspects of Skovoroda's thought. (The essay is contained in Skovoroda, *Tvori*, vol. II.) Two early surveys of Skovoroda and his philosophy were written by Khidzheu, "Grigorii Varsava [*sic*] Skovoroda. Istoriko-kriticheskii ocherk" [Grigorii Skovoroda. An historical-critical essay], *Teleskop* [Telescope] 26 (1835), 1–24, 151–178 [New York Public Library], and Father Superior Gavriil in the last volume of his six-volume *Istoriia filosofii* [History of philosophy], published in Kazan, 1839–1840 [Library of Congress]. Both works are factually unreliable and confined in their understanding of the scope and significance of Skovoroda's philosophy, but of value to the advanced student because they quote several pages of material then attributed to Skovoroda which today we must call interesting, but of at least questionable authenticity. Khidzheu also provides a glossary to clarify some of Skovoroda's more difficult words and expressions.

Despite a few inaccuracies and doubtful points of interpretation, N. Stelletskii's article, "Stranstvuiushchii ukrainskii filosof Grigorii Savvich Skovoroda" [Wandering Ukrainian philosopher Grigorii Savvich Skovoroda], *Trudy Kievskoi Dukhovnoi Akademii*, [Works of the Kiev Theological Academy] 2 (July, August 1894), 449–478, 608–629 [Harvard], is not much inferior to Ern in its discussion of Skovoroda's life. In fact, Stelletskii presents plausible bibliographical material not easily available elsewhere, although sometimes the sources of such information are stated poorly, if at all. F. A. Zelenogorskii, "Filosofiia Grigoriia Savvicha Skovorody, ukrainskago

filosofa xviii stoletiia" [Philosophy of Grigorii Savvich Skovoroda,
Ukrainian philosopher of the eighteenth century], *Voprosy filosofii
i psikhologii* [Questions of philosophy and psychology] 23 (1894),
197–234; 24 (1895), 281–315 [New York Public Library], always
scholarly and sometimes profound, is one of the finest short studies
of Skovoroda I have encountered. Fortunately Zelenogorskii eschews
a mere summary of Skovoroda's ideas; he is especially good on Skovoroda's indebtedness to Plato and Philo the Jew. A. S. Lebedev in
"G. S. Skovoroda kak bogoslov" [G. S. Skovoroda as a theologian],
Voprosy filosofii i psikhologii [Questions of philosophy and psy-
chology] 27 (1898), 170–177 [Library of Congress], says surprisingly little about Skovoroda, but will help scholars to locate Grigorii
Savvich within that ancient non-Russian patristic tradition with which
Skovoroda himself was so familiar.

The histories of Russian philosophy by E. Radlov, *Ocherk istorii
russkoi filosofii* [Study of the history of Russian philosophy] (Peterburg [*sic*], 1920) [Princeton] and Gustav Shpet, *Ocherk razvitiia
russkoi filosofii* [Study of the development of Russian philosophy]
(Petrograd, 1922) [Northwestern] do not view Skovoroda as a profound or original thinker. If I think these scholars are less than fair
to Skovoroda, I must admit I found their tone refreshing in contrast
to the storms of adulation so often encountered in reading about
him. Radlov, and especially Shpet, have moments of keen analysis
of certain features of Skovoroda's thought. V. V. Zenkovsky, *A History of Russian Philosophy*, trans. George L. Kline, 2 vols. (New
York: Columbia University Press; London: Routledge & Kegan Paul,
1953), is more reliable than Radlov and Shpet as a guide to Skovoroda's life and philosophy. Zenkovsky is respectful of Skovoroda and
writes about him with erudition and philosophic insight. He is also
strikingly successful in defining Skovoroda's relationship to the various patterns of Russian thought which emerged during the eighteenth
century. Professor Kline has presented an excellent translation of
Zenkovsky's *History* to the English-speaking world, but for shades
of expression and, above all, several useful footnotes eliminated in

the English translation I recommend the original version: V. V. Zenkovskii, *Istoriia russkoi filosofii* [A History of Russian Philosophy], 2 vols. (Paris, 1948–1950).

I am all but at a loss to comment upon I. A. Tabachnikov's contribution to V. E. Evgrafov et al., *Istoriia filosofii v SSSR* [History of Philosophy in the USSR], 5 vols. (Moscow, 1968–   ). Tabachnikov writes with intelligence, and since he participated in the 1961 publication of Skovoroda's works he must surely know Skovoroda's philosophy. Hence, at times, I wonder if Tabachnikov actually believes his own presentations of Skovoroda's thought. Not only does Tabachnikov view Skovoroda through Marxist philosophical categories which are usually alien to the spirit of Skovoroda's own work, but he also makes Skovoroda an active pioneer in the discovery of these concepts! When Tabachnikov tells us that Skovoroda was a devotee of science and a radical social thinker, he *lies*, as he does by citing on p. 409 of his first volume (from Khidzheu, "Grigorii Skovoroda," pp. 160–161) the following passage, changing Skovoroda's meaning by omitting words in the original which I have retained and placed in italics: "*Are you a horse? bear riders! Are you an ox? wear your yoke! A borzoi? chase animals! A hunter? kill bears!* . . . Everyone should recognize his people, and in his people, himself. Are you a Russian? be one: *believe in Orthodoxy, serve the tsarina truly, love your brother passionately*. Are you a Pole? be a Pole! Are you a German? act as a German! A Frenchman? act as a Frenchman! A Tatar? act as a Tatar! Everything is good in its place and in its measure, and everything that is beautiful is clean, natural, i.e., not false, not amalgamated, but existing in its own way." A shameful performance!

In this essay I did not cite Dmitrii Chizhevskii, "Filosofiia G. S. Skovorody (1722–1794)" [Philosophy of G. S. Skovoroda (1722–1794)], *Put* [Path] 19 (1930), 23–56 [New York Public Library], but wish to call it to the reader's attention at this time. Chizhevskii analyzes the relationship between Skovoroda's dialectical-symbolical method and the actual concepts of his philosophy, and he is especially informative on the sources of Skovoroda's thought in ancient philosophy, early church theology, and other subjects. Chizhevskii discusses Skovoroda's unique style and the symbolical exposition displayed in his dialogs. The author also draws useful parallels between Skovoroda and his contemporary thinkers of the West.

N.B. Not until this manuscript was in a stage of advanced preparation for publication did the following dissertation come to my attention: Stephen Patrick Scherer, *The Life and Thought of Russia's First Lay Theologian, Grigorij Savvič Skovoroda (1722–1794)*, Ph.D. dissertation, Department of History, Ohio State University, 1969, under the advisership of Michael W. Curran. Scherer's study is most commendable and in published form should be of great interest to students of Russian intellectual history.

Vladimir Soloviev's Christian State in the Christian Society

EDWARD C. BOCK

HANS KOHN ACCLAIMS Vladimir Soloviev as "Russia's foremost philosopher"[1] and "the greatest philosopher Russia has produced."[2] Avrahm Yarmolinsky is slightly more specific; he calls Soloviev "Russia's greatest systematic philosopher."[3] Several Roman Catholic authors regard him as the Russian Newman.[4] This designation is not always given to Soloviev for the reason Zouboff insinuates, namely that Catholic authors wish to make him a thorough Roman. There is in fact a close parallelism between Soloviev and Newman. Both were what might be called theological philosophers, expressing what Zenkovsky designates "the

[1] Hans Kohn, *Pan Slavism* (New York: Alfred A. Knopf, Vintage Books, 1960), p. 221.

[2] Hans Kohn (ed.), *The Mind of Modern Russia* (New York: Harper and Row, Harper Torchbooks, 1962), p. 27.

[3] Avrahm Yarmolinsky, *Road to Revolution* (New York: Collier Books, 1962), p. 27.

[4] Peter P. Zouboff (ed.), *Vladimir Solovyev's Lectures on Godmanhood* (Poughkeepsie, N. Y.: Harmon Printing House, 1944), p. 25.

exhibition of Christianity in the form of philosophy."[5] Both
were idealists, and, above all, both eventually became convinced
advocates of the primacy of Peter.

This essay will consider Soloviev's ideal Christian Society, his
arguments against liberalism, rationalism, socialism, and positivism. As far as possible, it will attempt to draw parallels between
Soloviev and Western Christian thought. It will place Soloviev,
an intellectual giant, between the Slavophiles and the Westernizers.

Much has been written about the Slavophiles and the Westernizers, so much that many students of Russian history think
the Russian intelligentsia was clearly divided into these two categories. However, as Soloviev's ideas evolve, it becomes increasingly clear that a small middle group evolved a system of its
own. In the case of Soloviev, it was not a system for Russia
only, but for the world, a system neither exactly Pan-Slavic nor
precisely Western, but an amalgamation of both.

Vladimir Sergeievich Soloviev was born in Moscow on January 16, 1853, and died on the estate of Prince Sergei Trubetskoi
on July 31, 1900. He was strongly influenced by family tradition. He admired his father, historian Sergei Mikhailovich
Soloviev, who between 1851 and 1879 authored the twenty-
six-volume *History of Russia since the Oldest Times.* He was
certain that his grandfather, the priest Mikhail Soloviev, "was
in direct communication with God."[6] His mother was Poliksena

---

[5] V. V. Zenkovsky, *A History of Russian Philosophy,* trans. from the
Russian by George L. Kline (New York: Columbia University Press;
London: Routledge and Kegan Paul, 1953), II: 472.

[6] Zouboff, *Solovyev on Godmanhood,* p. 11.

Skovoroda, a relative of Gregorii Skovoroda, the renowned Ukrainian philosopher who taught that everyone should lead an upright life and find happiness in an inner peace based on self-knowledge and self-sacrifice.

After the completion of his primary education at home and his secondary education at the Fifth Moscow Gymnasium, Vladimir entered the University of Moscow at the age of fifteen. For the first two years he studied mathematics and physics; then he changed to history and philosophy and completed his education with theology. The latter course was taken at the Moscow Theological Academy simultaneously with the classes in history and philosophy at Moscow University. He had a broad base for his philosophy.

While at the university, Soloviev found the philosophical basis for his concept of a universal, spiritual unity in Spinoza. During this period he fluctuated between faith in Christianity and atheism; following philosophy ranging from socialism to nihilism. He studied not only Spinoza but also John Stuart Mill, Kant, Schopenhauer, Darwin, Spencer, Fichte, Schelling, Hegel, Comte, Plato, the Fathers of the Church, Buddhism, and the other Eastern religions. Of the Fathers of the Church, he was specifically influenced by Augustine of Hippo and his doctrine concerning will and grace. It should be remembered that the Western Roman Church bestows the title of Doctor of Grace upon Augustine and bases her doctrine of grace upon his thesis. By 1872, under these influences, Soloviev had developed his own system of philosophy-theology, with but one basic change in the 1880's. This change was his conviction of the primacy of Peter. Soloviev died in communion with the Russian Orthodox Church and was buried in accordance with Russian rite, but as late as February 18, 1896, he participated in a Uniat service.[7]

Before his death in 1900, caused in no small part by overwork, he had written nine volumes on his philosophic-theologic system, plus four volumes of correspondence and one volume of poetry. His poems were devoted to his mystical experiences, to world-soul, and to eternal womanhood.

In order to understand any philosophic system, it is imperative to have a clear concept of the terminology the author employs. Many of the sharp misunderstandings and violent conflicts in philosophy and theology could be avoided if there were agreement on terminology and definitions, but such does not seem to be the case. Therefore, an attempt is made to understand the basic definitions of Soloviev's system. The terminology considered is indispensable in the analysis of his system on Church and State.

Soloviev defines religion as "the reunion of man and the world with the unconditional and integral principle. That principle, as integral and as all-embracing, excludes nothing, and therefore the true union with it, the true religion cannot exclude, or suppress, or forcibly subject to itself any element whatever, any living force either in man or in his universe."[8] For Soloviev religion is the focal point of all reality and possesses an all-embracing importance. He follows this norm in every area of his system, so frequently that often one wonders whether he is not more theologian than philosopher. Soloviev's term *Absolute* is frequently used in the sense of total unity, but Soloviev uses it with two meanings, as synonymous with the term *God*, but also

[7] Ibid., pp. 25–28.
[8] Ibid., p. 86.

to signify a duality, that of idea and that of matter. When he uses the term as total unity, Soloviev attempts to save himself from pantheism with a very subtle distinction: although God is the essential unity of all reality, He must also exist in himself and for himself, Soloviev writes.[9] In order to further avoid pantheism and rationalism, he states that the existence of God cannot be deduced by reason. Soloviev argues that the law of causality, as used by Aristotle and Saint Thomas Aquinas, can only point out to man that God is probable.

Soloviev uses the term *being* with the same connotation as has Plato—an awareness of self. Yet later in his works he seems to expand this initial definition: "In other words, a being, as such, is necessarily at one and the same time an atom [Epicurus], a living force (a monad) [Leibnitz], and an idea [Plato]."[10]

Soloviev defines man in the following manner: "Man combines in himself all possible opposites, which can be reduced to one great polarity between the unconditional and the conditional, between the absolute and eternal essence, and the transitory phenomenon or appearance. Man is at once divinity and nothingness."[11] His concept of reality is almost identical to its definitions by Plato, Spinoza, and Hegel. Before man is able to know reality outside of self, he must become aware of it as an idea in himself. The foundations of reality are forces (Hegelian)—being acting upon being and, in turn, being acted upon.

Finally, consideration must be given to Soloviev's concept of history, for it will help in understanding his Christian Society. Very few, if any, authorities have shown the influence of a philosopher's idea of history upon his system; ordinarily it is considered an influence upon history of philosophy. In the case of

[9] Ibid., p. 137.   [10] Ibid., p. 128.   [11] Ibid., p. 173.

Soloviev, his theory of history and historical causality aids in understanding his entire system as well as his Christian Society. The meaning and the goal of history for this eminent Russian philosopher coincide with the meaning and the goal of society. It is the messianic idea of the kingdom of God which progresses throughout the life of mankind and, of course, is governed by Divine Providence. The goal of history is identified with the objective of Christianity, which is the unity of mankind in a duality, one of faith and one of society.

In his law for the division of historical functions, he seems to be somewhat influenced by the ideas of Johann Gottfried von Herder. He, however, proceeds further than Herder. The law for the division of historical functions states that one culture, one nation, can realize only one universal idea, perform one historical act. He uses the example of Judaism which could not progress into the concept of Christianity. Judaism developed one universal concept, monotheism; Buddhism, self-purification; and Greek culture, the ideal cosmos. Christianity took the three universal ideas thus developed and produced the ideal unity of mankind, found in Christ, the God-man. Finally, Soloviev agrees with Hegel that the historical order and the logical order coincide in content.

What did Soloviev think about nationalism, liberalism, socialism, and positivism? He denounced all of these. He denounced nationalism in several ways. From his ideas of universal unity and universal religion, it may be concluded that he inherently opposed nationalism. However, he also made positive statements against nationalism. Soloviev argued against those who said that Russia had a God-given role or a prerogative to world leadership. He wrote: "When one ascribes to any nation a monopoly of the absolute truth, then nationality becomes an idol the worshipping of which is based upon a falsehood and leads to a moral and then to a material catastrophe . . . For a true and farsighted patriotism, the most essential, even the only essential question, is not the question of Russia's might but that of Russia's sins."[12]

Every nation has something to offer to the development and greatness of any other nation. Thus, "only through the closest internal and external ties with Europe can Russia become great."[13] Why? In his essay in praise of Peter the Great he presents a partial answer: "The recognition of universal interdependence made Russia a truly Christian nation."[14] Nationalism for Soloviev ignores the moral character and the ethical quality of a nation: "The greatest representatives of Russian literature have shown themselves to be free of all national exclusiveness. They were deeply affected by all that was good among other peoples, and they condemned all that was bad among us, the very aspects of Russian life which so enchant our obscurantists."[15] He then enumerates many examples from Russian literature to exemplify Western influences upon Russia. It was this tremendous influence of the West which for him formed a "Russian universalist awareness."[16]

Soloviev's principal philosophical argument against nationalism, however, was derived from nature: "As long as the state means everything, an ordering of human existence becomes

[12] V. S. Soloviev, "Against the Slavophils," in Hans Kohn (ed.) *The Mind of Modern Russia*, p. 220.

[13] Ibid., p. 219.

[14] V. S. Soloviev, "Peter's Reforms," in *The Mind of Modern Russia*, p. 230.

[15] Soloviev, "Against the Slavophils," p. 223.

[16] Ibid., p. 225.

meaningless."[17] Nationalism opposed his entire system of philosophy, for under nationalism man could not return to the universal unity in God. Nationalism theoretically resisted his entire
concept of society and more so his universal Christian Society.
Nationalism challenged the very basis of "Christ's chief com-
mandment—to make the active love of one's neighbor the basis
of all social life."[18] Christ's kingdom upon earth meant one
spiritual society and one secular society. The kingdom of the
world must be subjected to the kingdom of God, but for Soloviev
this was a spiritual subjugation.

There was, however, a certain type of nationalism which was
permissible. Soloviev uses the example of the prophets of the Old
Testament to clarify this: "Jonah preached the will of Jehovah
to the pagans of Nineveh; Isaiah and Jeremiah heralded the
coming revelation as the banner of the nations, to which all nations shall flow. Yet the Jewish prophets were at the same time
really the greatest patriots, fully permeated with the national
idea of Judaism; precisely because they were completely permeated with it, they had to understand it as universal, as predestined
for all men."[19]

Soloviev does not look favorably upon either the French Revolution or European liberalism. According to him, liberalism was
an evil result of the French Revolution. To him "the power of
the monarchy and feudal lords was merely replaced with the
power of capital and of the bourgeoisie,"[20] and this was the only
result of the revolution. He contends that it was absolutely mean-

---

[17] Soloviev, "Peter's Reforms," p. 213.
[18] Ibid.
[19] Zouboff, *Solovyev on Godmanhood*, p. 138.
[20] Ibid., p. 80.

ingless, for it did not give equality of powers: "The principle of equality, of equality of rights, proved to be real only for those who at the given historical moment possessed power."[21] He argues that liberalism of this kind is unnecessary for this reason as well as for the fact that its theoretical goals of equality, freedom, and brotherhood can only be attained through genuine Christianity.

In line with the theories of a Roman Catholic contemporary, Bishop Wilhelm von Ketteler of Mainz, Soloviev's conclusive argument against liberalism is that it opened the door for socialism. Just as liberalism seized power from the upper middle class, so socialism sought the seizure of power for the "have-not" class, the proletariat. Essentially the "have-not" class seeks the equalization of material welfare through socialism. What is wrong with this objective? Soloviev replies that man has natural rights besides material rights, and socialism does not recognize these. According to Soloviev, man seeks his own good: this is the ultimate goal of socialism, but socialism has no moral value, and a moral value is necessary in society. Soloviev further contends that the goal of socialism has no moral value, because justice in the moral sense is a certain limitation of one's rights in favor of the rights of others. He therefore concludes that socialism does not strive for justice. Socialism is true, he argues, insofar as it demands social truth, but the means it proposes are incorrect. Socialistic means are based upon the "egoism of individuals," but the means for society should be based upon self-denial and love, or charity. Soloviev felt everyone must sacrifice his exclusive will, and this is only possible in the recognition of God.

[21] Ibid.

Few would argue with the statement that man seeks his own ends. It seems that the weakness of Soloviev's argument is his analysis of the moral character of socialism, and this analysis depends upon the acceptance of Soloviev's definition of justice. In his definition of justice, no distinction is made between justice and charity; this is rather strange for a Christian. On the purely natural level, he leaves no room for the attainment of justice, since this fits very logically into his system of a universal religion and its necessity. For him there is no need for man to strive after justice for in man's adherence to Soloviev's religion justice would automatically evolve. In the Christian religion of his dreams, self-denial is the essential moral factor. His conclusion is that one who has no religious principles cannot be just.

Soloviev presents another argument in this manner:

By nature men are not equal among themselves because they do not possess equal powers; and as a result of the inequality of their powers, they necessarily find themselves in a state of forced subjection one to another; consequently, by nature they are not free either; finally by nature men are strange and inimical towards each other —natural humanity by no means represents a brotherhood. If, thus, the realization of the truth is impossible on the ground of given natural conditions in the kingdom of nature, then it is possible only in the kingdom of grace, that is to say, on the basis of the moral principle, as the unconditional or divine.[22]

However, this Russian philosopher sees some good in socialism, which he turns into an argument for his thesis: "Socialism logically leads to the recognition of the necessity of the unconditional principles of life, that is, to the acknowledgment of religion."[23] He concludes that socialism demands justice and social

[22] Ibid., pp. 85–86.
[23] Ibid., p. 85.

truth. Since these cannot be attained by natural means, socialism inadvertently but logically demands religion.

Adhering to his principle of opposition to all modern systems of thought, Soloviev denounces the Enlightenment of the eighteenth century with its proclamation of the rights and powers of human reason. He argues that reason is only a means of knowledge, not its content. Rationalism and positivism posit truth as the given fact—that which occurs or happens. Soloviev replies that truth has its own reality, since an individual phenomenon is acknowledged as true only in its relationship with the whole which is God. Although man knows reality only when he becomes aware of it as an idea in himself, reality exists without man knowing it. Because Soloviev's very system is essentially theocentric and mystical it denies any possibility of positivism.

Other concepts of Soloviev's which must be understood in order to comprehend the meaning of his Christian Society are here briefly summarized. Human nature in itself is evil, and it has only divine significance. The law of nature is the struggle for existence. This is all shown, he argues, by the fact that though a man is well fed and at the same time his lower passions are satisfied, he still struggles for mental and moral supremacy over his fellow men. Thus the fundamental evil in man's nature is egoism. Why make such a fuss about freedom, he asks, when every act of the human will is by its nature free?[24]

In "The Christian State and the Christian Society" Soloviev defines his Christian Society and presents arguments for his ideal.[25] All Christians will agree with him that the focal point of

[24] Ibid., p. 184.
[25] Vladimir Soloviev, "Vom Christlichen Staat und der Christlichen Gesellschaft," in *Die Religiösen Grundlagen des Lebens*, tr. from

world history is the coming of Christ; pre-Christian history looks forward to Christ, and, since Christ, it emanates from him. Following the Gospels, Christians take the words of Christ in their literal sense, as expressive of the goal of history: "Teach ye all nations, and baptize them . . ." However, from this generalization through the specific means to attain such a goal, many Christian thinkers would differ with Soloviev.

He makes a fine distinction between the perfection of an individual and of mankind. The perfection of individuals would not perfect society, from Soloviev's point of view, because he argues that society is not a total of equal and independent units. That individuals are not equal in abilities of mind and will would not be a point of argument with other Christian philosophers or theologians. Many, however, would disagree with Soloviev that, though each unit in society were Christlike, society would not be totally Christianized. It would seem that in this ideal Soloviev shows Platonistic influences. He wishes for a perfect, spiritualized mankind, which in turn would perfect each individual. Western Christian thinkers would disagree: the individual must perfect himself before society is improved. They would, however, agree with him that "the perfection of society through the direct effort of a perfect person is impossible." They would agree with his principle that "in order to renew the whole of mankind, Christianity must not only permeate the person but every element of society." In his analysis of the importance of Christ as the all-true and perfect being there is common agreement among Chris-

Russian into German by N. Hoffmann (Leipzig: Verlag von Oswald Mutze, 1907), pp. 140–156. All of the paraphrases and quotations in the rest of the paper are from this source.

tians. There is also agreement with Soloviev's basic principle of society and state: "Just as divinity was united to humanity in Christ, so the divine unity must be expressed in the free union of the church with the state."

The ideal unity between civil and ecclesiastical authority in a Christian society was the ideal of the medieval West. Soloviev himself takes up this aspect in later discussions, but it should be noted that this general concept is almost identical to Pope Boniface VIII's bull, *Unam sanctam*, of November 18, 1302. Besides the close identity of the basic principle of Soloviev with *Unam sanctam*, there is a remarkable parallelism in their concepts of the ideal Christian society. The similarity does not hold true when Soloviev shows his Platonic and Russian influences. Nor does it hold true in Boniface's subordination of secular power to spiritual power; only the Christian idealism is identical.

This close parallelism is specifically noted in Soloviev's concept of subordination. He opposes an unlimited despotism but maintains that the state must demand subordination on the part of its subjects for protection from external forces. "It has always been that way and always will be, and the only difference lies in the character and in the form of this subordination." He points out that subordination must not be as it was in the pre-Christian empires, where "children did not belong to their fathers, and captives had no rights from the conqueror: everyone was obliged to absolute submission." As in the East so in the West only the strong had rights, for the axiom, might is right, was the principle at the time. However, Soloviev admits that the West attempted to displace might with law, and Rome succeeded fairly well in this attempt. Yet the Roman legal system was still based upon force. His analysis of pre-Christian East and West was: "For the Eastern people its despotic empire showed itself as an unavoidable evil, as one of the oppressive and unavoidable conditions of mortal life—nothing more. But for Western paganism with its purely human religion the State was looked upon as the incarnation of all human understanding and all human truth; in it they saw the highest norm as the highest goal of their lives. And, remember this, the goal was completely reached. A perfect state was sought, the all-inclusive, the invincible, all-conquering state —the Roman World Empire."

For the reader, the question that remains unanswered throughout Soloviev's system is: Will the perfect Christian state in a perfect Christian society need protection from external forces? Since this perfect society was universal for Soloviev, where would evil external forces come from? He never answers this question. Another question: Is subordination necessary for protection from internal disturbing forces? He answers this indirectly when he deals with crime. It might be pointed out that Soloviev is logical in the admission of crime in his Christian Society. He never denies the possibility that an individual can commit sin against society. However, he implies that church and state cannot be wrong if they follow his prescriptions. This again emphasizes the influence of Plato on Soloviev; the general impresses itself on the particular, the ideal forms the individual. Thus the perfect Christian Society perfects the individual.

What is the difference between the pagan and the Christian state? The pagan state had itself as its goal. "The Christian state, however, recognizes a higher goal than itself, which is given it by religion and is represented by the church. . . . The Christian state finds its highest goal and purpose in the kingdom of God."

Upon these principles Soloviev constructs his ideal Christian Society. He calls upon the state, not only to battle against the mad strength of the world (here "world" means anything non-Christian) under the banner of the Church, but also to lead the people from a purely secular life to the elevation of ecclesiastical ideals patterned upon the example and imitation of Christ. His Christian state has all of the essentials of a state but with different connotations and with a renewal in the "spirit of Christian truths."

There is one sovereign in his Christian state who has sovereignty not in the name of his own strength but in the name of the general welfare and in harmony with the laws of ecclesiastical authority. There is subjection in his Christian state, not as a result of slavery, but of conviction, free, and in the name of mutual effort, which the sovereign serves as well as the subjects. There are rights in his Christian state, but rights not founded upon "the limitless human egoism, but upon the moral infinity of humanity as a divine reality." There exists in his Christian state one law, not in the sense of a simple determination of actual relationships, but in the sense of "perfection after the idea of the highest truth." There is in his Christian state a supreme authority, yet "not as a deification of human free will, but as a special servitude to the will of God." . . . "The representative of strength in the Christian state is not the possessor of all right, as the pagan Caesar—it is essentially the supporter of all obligations of the Christian society in regard to the Church, that is, in regard to the work of God upon earth."

Secular power is rooted in the spiritual except for its source of power; however, it is completely independent of the spiritual power. "For that reason its mutual determination can only be a free and moral one based upon faith and truth." The authority of the Christian state is duty-bound to believe in the church. Its complete moral strength must be freely subordinate to the higher authority of the church, not in the sense that ecclesiastical authority interferes in secular affairs, but that the state itself subordinates its activity to the higher religious interests, never losing sight of the kingdom of God.

In the Christian West the Church once attempted to clothe itself in a secular form. In the Christian East the power of the state not only strove for secular power but very often took over ecclesiastical authority. In Soloviev's ideal, free theocracy, the state itself is permeated with Christian elements. The Church is involved in secular matters to the same degree that the state is involved in ecclesiastical ideals. As the state serves the higher, religious interest through a free servitude, it becomes ideal and spiritual. The religious interest, which flows from the Church and which the state, under the leadership of the Church, should serve, is based upon the following: (1) propagating Christianity in the world; (2) bringing peoples together peacefully within the realm of Christianity; and (3) constructing a society founded upon Christian ideals in every united people.

For an explanation of this last point, Soloviev uses a lengthy example on "the relations of the state and society to a criminal." This example also gives an excellent idea of how the Church fits into the social pattern. He claims that instead of the pagan principle of recompense, his Christian state would apply the Christian principle of compassion. Under this premise an understanding, not only for the crime and the sufferers from the crime,

but also for the criminal himself would be sought. While his
Christian state has the duty to protect itself from crime and is not
justified for failure in this respect, it also has the responsibility
for the "rebirth of the soul of the criminal."

The state should concern itself with the improvement and rebirth of the criminal as it assists in the healing of bodily ills. The
state builds hospitals and helps in a material manner the doctors
who are dedicated professionally to this problem. In the same
manner that the state concerns itself with the sick and battles
against disease, it must concern itself with the security of its
people and battle against crime. "As the concern of physical
healing is not brought about through a health police but through
a remedy, so in the normal state the concern for moral improvement is not brought about by a judge and captivity but through
the Church and its servants, to whom the state must give the
material opportunity to rehabilitate the criminal." This moral
rehabilitation by the Church begins with the criminal where the
effectiveness of the state ends. In regard to this "the Church
must have confidence as doctors have confidence in medical science." For Soloviev there are three items involved in the recognition and the investigation of every criminal: "(1) the illegality rooted in the ill will of the criminal—the sin or fault is here
included; (2) the injury inherent in one way or another in the
crime—for the one injured as well as for the entire society; (3)
the misfortune for the criminal himself as a man."

The state has a duty to uphold the law and to protect society
from dangerous members. Justice will be appeased in that regard
through the punishment of the criminal. For Soloviev "it is indispensable that the criminal lose his freedom and his citizen's

rights and be cut off from society." Although the first two points
will have been satisfied after the criminal regains his freedom,
the question concerning the criminal himself still remains.

To remedy the misfortune of the criminal, he must be handed
over to the Church for redemption. The Church should have no
part in the conviction and punishment of the criminal, but should
only concern itself "with his salvation, as if founded upon the
law of salvation." The Church should not be primarily concerned
with the illegality of the crime or with the criminal's responsibility. The Church should be concerned with every interior and
exterior association, with every physical and psychological aspect
which led the man to commit the crime. If the Church does not
have the strength to expunge these aspects, it can always diminish
them. If the Church cannot always heal the criminal of the world
and return him a reborn man, at least it can and should try to
place him in a better environment in order to free him from bad
influences and companions.

Without in the least denying the legality of every social and
private interest protected by the penal law and the police, it is
"absolutely necessary to add that the final sin of the Christian
state toward crime is its own moral cure, an objective in which
the state can serve the Church in its achievement." A similar
service of the state should be applied in the solution of other
problems. The state serves the Church insofar "as it exchanges
the principle of unity on the international plane for nationalism
and hostility," and "propagates Christian culture among barbaric
and uncivilized peoples, humbles the proud, disarms the covetous,
and aids those in servitude." From the Church the state receives
its high goals and the "positive purposes for its functions."

Only the Christian religion has given meaning and purpose to the state, since it has elevated itself above the state. "The higher the sun stands over the world, the more it warms and lights the world." As long as the state was everything, society was nothing. As soon as the purpose of life was placed above the state, "the living power of society was freed and servitude to the state came to an end."

In reality in the ancient world there was only one social class. This singular social class was divided into free citizens, landowners, and slaves who did all of the manual work; but in fact all of society was in a state of slavery to the absolute state. The members of that society had "no absolute goal for their basic life and knew nothing higher than the state and were devoured by it." Religion was under the complete control of the state. "All of society, its meaning, its matter and spirit, was ruled by the state and for the state."

Among Christians, religion is held higher than the state; through religion society is freed from the absolute authority of the state and the result is a free, independent society. Christianity gives all members of the Church an equal purpose in life. When they became Christians, the former slaves entered into the complex of society. In none of his works does Soloviev directly condemn slavery. For him the mere fact that a slave became a Christian, or was a Christian, made him equal to his fellow Christians, in an "equality in Christ." It seemed to be sufficient to be a member of the "God-man society" in order to be free. However, he does admit that this equality and freedom in Christianity is only in a potential state and must become a realization through the efforts of mankind itself. The individual, freed interiorly through the grace of Christ, must apply this freedom to the work of constructing the Christian Society.

To Soloviev human society is not simply a mechanical union of individual human beings. It is an independent whole and has its own life and its own organization. The lesson of Christianity is this: "that in the life of an organization of social strength the Christian element of moral solidarity or true brotherhood is brought into the picture."

The Western Church's idea about this is slightly different from Soloviev's. The Western doctrine of the Mystical Body of Christ has been the basic doctrine always in the concept of a Christian society. There is agreement that all are equal in Christ through grace. To the Western Church each individual is a unit in the entire body, and there is a mutual interdependence between the whole and each member and between the various members.

For Soloviev the construction of human society is "simply and perfectly ordered in its essential outline and fully reasonable." Human society must before all else stand firmly upon the earth, be certain of its material existence, and live a natural life. However, in this alone "the enduring life of mankind is not fulfilled and its purpose is not found in itself." Society must possess the means to change its life, to develop its strength, and to move itself. The terms of such movement, development, and progress will be worked out through civilization. Alone, the development and progress of civilized life would be "purposeless and foolish." Social progress, if it is to be energetic, must lead society to a determined, immediate, unconditional, worthy, and ideal aim. "Society must not only be alive and move itself; it must be based upon agriculture and through an artistic development must develop a higher goal with all its might." He tosses in this afterthought: "Labor in every endeavor is especially very worthwhile."

His Christian Society is divided into three classes which somewhat reflect Plato's division. The three classes are "the people in the narrow sense—the rural, essentially agricultural class; the class in towns; and finally the class of 'better people'—public servants, leaders of the people, generals; in other words: the village, the town, and the military."

These three principal elements of society were united in the ancient world through the absolutism of the state; Christianity has freed them, and the proposition of Christian "state-art" is rooted "in a legitimate manner to unite the Church and state."

The legitimate manner of this unity depends directly upon the class of "better people," the class that rules. They are the "leaders of society which govern the origin of every section." For the lowest class, "the people in the narrow sense," have always restrained themselves not only against the Church but against the state and the other classes. The lowest class has always "fulfilled its destiny, has distributed the soil to every need, and has thereby chosen its full solidarity with the higher religious and civic interests." The middle class is "only its own destiny and has in the duty of its function always followed the example of the higher class," and it is not "its fault if it did not receive a good example." In all "promises the 'better people' have not to this day conformed to their destiny."

In the establishment of a free theocracy the "better people" have an "honorable and heavily responsible role." Insofar as they bow freely before the authority of the Church, insofar as they receive the "unshakeable principles of truth and good, so the 'better people' must agree with these principles and work and strive under the protection of the state with all their social strength" for the highest goal of society. This objective has "no option or chance" and neither is it achieved purely by human efforts. This purpose will be irrevocably determined by the Church; the state will also observe it with its forceful organization. This end is also that which "Christian people desire in the depth of their souls." This goal is "the realization of that which, we believe, is the change of our human and secular reality into the pattern of Christian truth, the essence of God-manhood."

Soloviev's dream of a universal Christian Society which was to be ruled by one secular and one ecclesiastical authority was not a new ideal. It had been the ideal of Christian theologians and philosophers from the time of the Fathers of the Church. The realization of this ideal was attempted especially from approximately 800 to the end of the reign of Pope Boniface VIII in 1303. Soloviev points out the failure of this attempt and lays the blame for its failure upon the Roman Church insofar as it attempted to dominate secular power. He gives no assurance that his system would not end in the same manner, that is, in a power struggle between church and state.

Seemingly, after baptism there is no distinction for Soloviev between the natural tendencies in man and supernatural grace. Roman Catholicism maintains a distinction between the natural order and the supernatural to avoid pantheism, the very pit into which Soloviev falls. Despite Soloviev's very subtle argument about a distinction within the Absolute it is difficult to comprehend how he can avoid the label of pantheism. Furthermore, he assumes that Christian baptism makes all men essentially good. True, he recognizes the possibility of crime in his ideal society; however, he does not blame the criminal but the "physical and psychological aspects which led the man to crime." In his attempt toward realism, he seems to destroy his ideal. What will prevent civic or ecclesiastical authority from crime—from egoism, which he maintains destroyed the Western ideal? He does not solve this problem.

The primary value of Soloviev lies in the fact that he recognized a problem for society and attempted to solve it. It lies in the fact that in Russian intellectual history he stands philosophically between the Westernizers and the Slavophiles. He was not a Russian nationalist, but he believed in the brotherhood of man.

BIBLIOGRAPHY

Collingwood, R. G. *The Idea of History.* New York: Oxford University Press, Galaxy Books, 1956.

Karpovich, Michael. "Vladimir Soloviev on Nationalism." *The Review of Politics* 8 (April 1946): 183–191.

Kohn, Hans. *Pan-Slavism: Its History and Ideology.* 2nd rev. ed. New York: Alfred A. Knopf, Vintage Books, 1960.

———, ed. *The Mind of Modern Russia: Historical and Political Thought of Russia's Great Age.* New York: Harper and Row, Harper Torchbooks, 1962.

Laurin, J. "Vladimir Soloviev and Slavophilism." *The Russian Review* 20, no. 1 (Nov. 1960): 11–18.

Loesky, N. O. *A History of Russian Philosophy.* New York: Harmon Printing House, 1951.

Pfleger, Karl. "Soloviev: The Prophet of Divine Humanity." In *Wrestlers with Christ,* Translated from the German by E. I. Watkin. New York: Sheed and Ward, 1936.

Soloviev, Vladimir. *God, Man and the Church.* Translated by Donald Attwater. New York: Sheed and Ward, 1946.

Solowjew, Wladimir. *Das Lebensdrama Platons.* Translated from the Russian by Bertram Schmitt. Mainz: Mathias Grünewald Verlag, 1926.

———. *Die Rechtfertigung des Guten.* Stuttgart: Der Kommende Tag A. G. Verlag, 1922.

———. *Die Religiösen Grundlagen des Lebens.* Translated from the Russian by N. Hoffmann. Leipzig: Verlag von Oswald Mutze, 1907.

————. *Schriften zur Vereinigung der Kirchen und zur Universalen Theokratie.* Translated from the Russian by Rudolph Miller. 2 vols. Freiburg im Breisgau: Erich Wewel Verlag, 1957.

Yarmolinsky, Avrahm. *Road to Revolution.* New York: Collier Books, 1962.

Zenkovsky, V. V. *A History of Russian Philosophy.* 2 vols. Translated by George L. Kline. New York: Columbia University Press; London: Routledge and Kegan Paul, 1953.

Zouboff, Peter P., ed. *Vladimir Solovyev's Lectures on Godmanhood.* Poughkeepsie, N. Y.: Harmon Printing House, 1944.

Literary Censorship in Russia
And the Soviet Union

LEON I. TWAROG

THERE IS A RUSSIAN PROVERB which says, "Once you have joined the pack, even if you do not bark, the least you can do is to wag your tail." In a society where censorship is in effect and where the values of that society are protected and fostered by the imposition of this system of censorship, all are expected to bark or at least to wag. Furthermore, if the official *Weltanschauung* changes drastically overnight, it is important that one bark or wag at the right time.

As Alexander Solzhenitsyn points out in his novel *The Cancer Ward*, writers in the Soviet Union are very flexible and very sensitive. In fact, they know almost without asking exactly what is expected of them. In Solzhenitsyn's novel, the daughter of the party official Rusanov speaks of this wonderful flexibility that literary critics in the USSR seem to have in particular: "They used to say, 'There should be no conflicts in literature.' Now they talk about 'the false theory of no-conflicts.' If they differed among themselves, if some critics said the old thing and some said the new, it would be clear that something had changed. But they all begin to say the new thing, all together, all of a sudden, so you don't realize that anything has changed. The most important thing is to be sensitive to the times, and responsive to them. Then you won't be criticized."[1]

Russian literature has endured censorship for more than two and a half centuries. That is, both in tsarist Russia and in the Soviet Union writers who did not do so of their own free will were induced to be sensitive to the times and responsive to them, but often only after considerable criticism or literary surgery on the part of the censors. The systems in the tsarist and Soviet periods, however, differ in their aims and methods and in their effect on the literary creativity of the authors.

Tsarist Russia developed its system of censorship in the late eighteenth century when most of the other countries of Western Europe were already free of censorship.[2] To the end of the eight-

[1] Alexander I. Solzhenitsyn, *The Cancer Ward*, trans. Rebecca Frank (New York: Dell Publishing Co., 1969), p. 333.

[2] An extensive bibliographic survey of both prerevolutionary and Soviet literature dealing with the history of Russian censorship is to be found in a publication of the Academy of Sciences library in the U.S.S.R. See L. M. Dobrovol'skij, "Bibliograficheskij obzor dorevoljutsionnoj i sovetskoj literatury po istorii russkoj tsenzury" in *Trudy Biblioteki Akademii Nauk SSSR i Fundamental'noj Biblioteki Obshchestvennykh Nauk* (Moscow-Leningrad, Akademija Nauk, 1961), pp. 245–252. Two prerevolutionary scholars who contributed most to the interpretation and history of nineteenth-century literary censorship are A. M. Skabichevskij and M. Lemke. The following are their most important publications: A. M. Skabichevskij, *Ocherki po istorii russkoj tsenzury (1700–1863)* (St. Petersburg: F. F. Pavlenkov, 1892); M. Lemke, *Epokha tsenzurnykh reform (1859–1865)* (St. Petersburg, 1904); M. Lemke, *Ocherki po istorii russkoj tsenzury i zhurnalistiki XIX stoletija* (St. Petersburg, 1904); M. Lemke, *Nikolaevskie zhandarmy i*

eenth century, when publication in Russia was a government monopoly, the responsibility for censorship was vested first in the ecclesiastical authorities and then in the Academy of Sciences. The first private printing establishment was opened in St. Petersburg in 1771, but was permitted to publish only foreign books, and then only those that would not be harmful to Christian laws or to the government.

The Pugachev rebellion of 1773–1775 (a revolt of sufficient magnitude to threaten the Russian government), the French Revolution, and the spread of Freemasonry and liberal ideas in Russia in the late eighteenth century prompted the government in 1796 to set up special censorship committees at ports of entry for foreign books. Censors were appointed for work in the capital cities and later even in some of the smaller towns. In 1800 the government went so far as to prohibit the import of all foreign books. Although that regulation was rescinded in 1801, four months later it was again in force in modified form. An official censorship code, instituted in 1804, proposed not only to do away with books and pamphlets which were antimoral, but to give to the public books and works which would lead to the flowering of the mind, the development of good taste, and a proper way of life.

------

literatura 1826–1855 gg. (St. Petersburg, 1908). One American scholar, Sidney Monas, has made a particularly important contribution to the interpretation of censorship policy and practice under Nicholas I. See Sidney Monas, *The Third Section*, Russian Research Center Studies no. 42 (Cambridge, Mass.: Harvard University Press, 1961). For the nineteenth century a particularly good summary of censorship history and policy is to be found in the standard prerevolutionary Russian encyclopedia, *Entsiklopedicheskij slovar'*, 53 vols.: 37, part 2 (St. Petersburg: F. A. Brokgauz and I. A. Efron, 1903), 949–962.

With the revised code of 1826, censorship became the concern of the highest echelons of the government, the ministers of education and of internal and foreign affairs. The code, so strict it was called the "iron code," or "cast iron code," was a direct consequence of the Decembrist uprising of 1825. It stated that censorship ought to be concerned with "the education and the upbringing of the youth, and with directing public opinion in keeping with the political circumstances and views of the government." When the code was revised in 1828, a more moderate approach prevailed. Censorship was no longer intended to give specific direction to public opinion, but to prohibit the circulation of literary works, and to prohibit any of the other arts and crafts which could be construed as harmful to the faith (orthodoxy), to the throne (monarchy), and to the morals and personal integrity of the citizens.

The code of 1828 remained in effect through the 1850's. In 1863 censorship became the responsibility of the ministry of the interior, and in 1865 a law which remained in effect to 1905 abolished prepublication censorship for original works of more than 160 pages or translations of more than 320 pages. Prepublication censorship for all small books and brochures was continued as before. Periodical publications (including the so-called fat journals, where most of the important nineteenth-century writers published their masterpieces on the installment plan) could be freed from prepublication censorship only with the permission of the minister of the interior. By 1905 prepublication censorship was lifted for periodicals, but publishers were subject to prosecution for breaking the censorship rules.

The impact of tsarist censorship was felt mainly by the Russian intellectual community. With the exception of ecclesiastical literature, there was no real need for literary censorship until a Russian intelligentsia began to develop in the late eighteenth century. But, in a country where serfdom was in force until 1861, where the rule of the monarchs was absolute, any threat to the monarchy, whether through armed uprising or through the opposition of the intellectuals, would be met by the application of ever-stricter censorship codes. The victims of censorship in the late eighteenth century were those intellectuals and writers who were tainted with ideas coming from the West, ideas that could be construed as undermining the government in one way or another. The experience of two intellectuals, Novikov and Radishchev, illustrate the harsh measures the government could take.

Nikolai Ivanovich Novikov (1744–1818) was known for his enlightened tendencies and as the editor of several of the so-called satirical journals modeled after the English *Spectator* and others that flourished toward the end of the eighteenth century in Russia. In 1769 Novikov began publication of his first satirical journal, *The Drone*. Through its pages he actually engaged in a polemic with a journal edited by Catherine the Great. When the polemic got too sharp, in 1780, *The Drone* was closed by the government, but Novikov published several other satirical journals and a newspaper. He had his own printing plants at that time and operated a network of bookstores in the major cities. Approximately one-third of all the books published in Russia from 1779 to 1792 were published by Novikov or printed at his plants.

As a Freemason and a liberal, and as a person interested in raising the educational and intellectual level of the populace, Novikov was in constant conflict with the government. In 1792 he was arrested on charges that his bookstores were selling forbidden books, and that he conspired with revolutionary-minded masons. In the investigation that followed, the revolutionary charges could not be proven, and consequently Novikov could not be brought to trial for his transgressions. Nevertheless, on August 1, 1792, Catherine II signed an order in which it was stated that "although he did not reveal his secret projects, nevertheless there were enough of all those accusations set forth under the six counts to subject him 'according to the law to the most severe and merciless punishment.' However, Catherine, in keeping with that love of mankind which was so much a part of her, and wishing to leave him time to repent for his evil doings, limited herself to ordering 'that he be shut up for fifteen years in the Schlusselberg Fortress.'"[3]

In 1796, when Paul I came to the throne, Novikov was released from prison, but by that time he was a broken man and he never fully recovered from his ordeal.

The second case is that of another member of the intelligentsia, of the so-called Voltairian group, Alexander Nikolaevich Radishchev (1749–1802). As a man who had been exposed to the leading ideas of Western scholars at Leipzig University, Radishchev was one of the very few Russians of the time who was totally imbued with Western ideas, and seeking to apply them to Russian reality. His book, *A Journey from Petersburg to Moscow*, which purported to describe a fictitious journey but gave the author the opportunity to comment on the nature of Russian life and Russian society, proved to be his undoing, primarily because many of his readers could identify themselves or their friends as the models for characters in the volume. The book was ready

---

[3] Skabichevskij, *Ocherki po istorii russkoj tsenzury*, p. 53.

toward the end of 1788, that is, just a few months prior to the French Revolution which was to shake all the monarchies of the world.

The *Journey* was submitted to the censor in St. Petersburg and was returned with some notations, but with the approval of Chief of Police Ryleev who signed his approval without looking at the book. Radishchev's printer refused to print it, despite the fact that it had officially been passed by the censor, and Radishchev published it himself. The volume immediately became a cause célèbre. Catherine read it and commented on it in some detail. She concluded her analysis with the statement that the author ought to be brought to trial. He had obviously bypassed some procedures, had portrayed Russia in a very bad light, and was imbued with the ideas of the French Revolution. An investigation was begun. Ryleev was the real culprit for he had initially passed the book, but he threw himself at Catherine's feet and she forgave his indiscretion.

With Radishchev things were much more difficult. He became flustered and proceeded to burn his own copies of the book, including the copy that had been signed by the censor. When an investigating commission asked him why he wanted to do away with censorship, he answered, in a manner reminiscent of some confessions by recent Soviet writers: "I admit my error. I thought that one could do without it (censorship), but now I see on the basis of my own experience that it is all the more useful, that if it will exist as our maker of laws has deigned to establish it, then it will really save many of those who like me happen to err in their thinking, from that ruination into which I have flung myself really because of weak intellect."[4]

[4] Ibid., p. 59.

For his crimes Radishchev was given the death penalty, commuted to banishment to Siberia for ten years. In 1797 Paul I permitted Radishchev to return to an estate near Moscow, although under strict police supervision. In 1801, upon the death of Paul, he was permitted to return to St. Petersburg.

The cases of Radishchev and Novikov are in no way extraordinary for that time in Russian history. Particularly after the French Revolution, the government was very much on the alert to stamp out anything that could be construed as directed against the monarchy. In 1793 alone some 18,656 copies of "harmful" books were burned by order of the censors. Catherine the Great took a personal interest in all of these matters. As an author, she understood perhaps better than others the dangers inherent in freedom of expression.

In the nineteenth century, Count Alexander Benckendorff, who won the complete confidence of the tsar by crushing the ill-fated Decembrist uprising on December 14, 1825, was appointed head of the secret police in the so-called Third Section and given the responsibility of enforcing censorship regulations—the "cast iron code." He considered it his personal duty to seek out and harass the leading literati of the day. The major writers of the period, Pushkin, Lermontov, Gogol, and Griboedov were all subjected to his arbitrariness.[5]

The case of Alexander Pushkin, the most celebrated Russian poet of the nineteenth century, can be taken as an example. Pushkin had been a close friend of many of the Decembrists, but at the time of the uprising he was already in exile and consequently did not participate. Nevertheless, Benckendorff treated him as if

[5] The period of Nicholas I, 1825–1855, is discussed in detail by Sidney Monas in *The Third Section*.

he were one of the Decembrists. In the case of Pushkin, for special reasons, the tsar *himself* decided to be his personal censor, which meant that over and above the usual apparatus of censorship, and Count Benckendorff, Pushkin was forced to submit all of his material to the tsar before it could be printed. From the correspondence between Pushkin and Benckendorff, and from the annotations Benckendorff and the tsar made on the manuscripts submitted by Pushkin, there is no question but that every one of Pushkin's works was perused most carefully by both Benckendorff and the tsar.

In one instance Benckendorff reviewed Pushkin's drama, *Boris Godunov*, for Nicholas I in rather detailed fashion, from both the ideological and the literary point of view. The tsar made some of his own notations, including one that is unusual because it implies a censorship of literary form. The tsar said that he felt "Pushkin's aim would be fulfilled if, with the requisite changes, he made his comedy over into a historical novelette or novel in the manner of Walter Scott."

Pushkin objected to this change in form but did make the required changes in content and again the drama was returned to him with the same suggestions. Finally, in 1830, four years after he had originally submitted his drama for consideration, he was given permission to publish *Boris Godunov,* which then appeared in 1831.

Some of Pushkin's best works did not appear in his lifetime. *The Bronze Horseman*, a narrative poem about Peter the Great and St. Petersburg and one of his acknowledged masterpieces, was written in 1833 and submitted for censorship, but was not printed until after his death in 1837. Even after his death Pushkin was not safe from the censors. Those friends who spoke too warmly about him in obituaries were reprimanded and some portions of the articles were deleted by the censors. Mikhail Lermontov was sent into exile because in a poem he blamed the government for Pushkin's death. Immediately after Pushkin's death, the tsar agreed to a complete posthumous edition of Pushkin's work, but only on condition that material he personally had formerly indicated as being unsuitable was deleted, and only if once again everything was edited very carefully. Two censors were assigned this special task under the direction of Minister Uvarov, but through the intercession of the poet Zhukovsky, the tsar finally relented and permitted the publication of the complete works without any changes.[6]

One can hardly speak of the problems of censorship during the reign of Nicholas I (1825–1855) without also mentioning the difficulties encountered by the literary journals which happened to print something the censors did not like. *The European* was closed because the censor insisted that the editor was using some kind of Aesopian language in one of his articles, and that he was really advocating revolution. The editor was placed under police surveillance. The *Moscow Telegraph* was closed in 1834, because, in a review of a highly nationalistic and one must say bad play entitled *The Hand of Most High Has Saved the Fatherland*, the reviewer had a sentence that read, "Kukol'nik's new drama grieves us." The editor had to travel from Moscow to St. Petersburg to explain this sentence, and, even though he had a good explanation and was freed, nevertheless the journal was closed. The *Telescope* was closed in 1836 because it published the now famous philosophical letter of Chaadaev about which Russian intellectuals still argue today, a philosophical discourse on

[6] Skabichevskij, *Ocherki po istorii russkoj tsenzury*, p. 273.

the nature of Russia and its mission in the world. The publisher was exiled. Chaadaev was declared insane and put under house arrest. A doctor came to visit him daily, and he was free to receive visitors. Eventually he agreed to write a retraction of sorts which he did under the title of "Apology of a Madman" and was declared sane again.

However, as Monas points out, there was not a single case of treasonable literature, per se, to 1848: "Reprimands, rebukes, fines, bans, surveillance, temporary exile, even short-term imprisonment in the guardhouse, implied something short of the criminal act, implied that the victim was at least basically loyal to the regime and could and would mend his ways if punished in proper paternal fashion. The case of greatest doubt, certainly, was that of Chaadaev, and it was characteristically resolved by having him declared insane."[7]

Censorship became increasingly restrictive in the last years of Nicholas's reign, 1845–1855, because the revolutions of 1848 in Europe increased the fear of the Russian government that it, too, would be overthrown. Dostoevsky was sent off to exile simply because he had been present at a reading of Belinsky's letter to Gogol (which could never have been printed since it criticized the government). Turgenev suffered because of his obituary of Gogol in 1852. In 1852, all discussion of Gogol in the press was forbidden.

After 1855 a few new journals were founded, and the requirement for prepublication censorship of periodical literature was abolished in the capital cities, though not in the provincial press. It often happened, however, that articles banned in the provincial press appeared in the capital cities with the notation that

[7] Monas, *The Third Section*, p. 196.

they were being so presented precisely because they had been banned in the provinces, even though they might be of little interest in the big cities. By the late nineteenth century there were many topics that could not be mentioned at all, even though they might be of great interest to the public. For example, newspapers could report student disorders, and hunger, cholera, or peasant uprisings only as official communiqués, without commentary.

Books banned in Russia in the nineteenth century are a special category. Although some were noted by scholars prior to 1917, it was not until 1962 that a well-documented list of such books appeared.[8] The list consists of 248 volumes which, during the period 1826–1904, were legally printed, but then were either banned and stopped in press, or confiscated after they had been put on the market.[9]

Most of the 248 volumes are original works, longer than 160 pages, or translations of more than 320 pages. An analysis of the statements made by the censors about each of the works and of the further comments of the censorship committee reveals that in almost all cases the books were banned because they could be interpreted as opposing the Russian way of life of the nineteenth century and fostering distrust of monarchic government. Two books dealing with the United States serve as examples of the thinking of the censors. *A History of the American United States*, by K. F. Nieman, translated from the German in 1873, was banned because the author sympathized too much with the Republicans. By implication he rejected the principles of monarchic government. The censor admitted that the pages in question were

[8] Lev Mikhailovich Dobrovol'skij, *Zapreshchennaja kniga v Rossii 1825–1904* (Moscow: Izdatel'stvo vsesojuznoj knizhnoj palaty, 1962).
[9] Ibid., pp. 3–4.

quotations from the Republicans (Americans) involved, but, even so, he said the book could have an effect on unthinking individuals and for that reason it was banned.[10]

Another, an original work by S. A. Shashkov entitled *The Feminist Movement in America*, was published in 1875. The censor had found something wrong with 55 of the 245 pages. The minister of internal affairs described the book as follows:

This work contains a description of the various phases of family life, and the social position of women in America, a description of the struggle of the women in this country for social and political equality, and the contemporary situation in America as regards the question of female emancipation. Shashkov obviously considers the points he is making to be not exclusively local, that is, American, but as applying to all mankind, universal. Sometimes the author even turns his thoughts to Russia, from which one can conclude that he is writing not only about America but that he also has in mind our fatherland. . . . Besides the general nature of its overwhelming sympathy with the female movement, this work of Shashkov's does praise representative government, to be sure, without any confrontation with the monarchic system, but with a direct indication of the superiority of the representative system. If one takes into account the fact that the book already mentioned is directed toward the censure and the weakening of the bases of the family union, and that in general this book contains ideas that are not in agreement with the structure of our state and society, it is impossible not to admit that its distribution would be harmful.[11]

Because no system is totally effective, human nature being what it is, apparently at least a few copies of all those editions officially ordered destroyed did survive. It seems that the police in charge of the burning would always save several copies, often as many as

10 Ibid., p. 107.
11 Ibid., p. 121.

fifty, which they could sell to collectors as rare books for as much as five hundred rubles, a huge sum for that time. In some instances, more money was realized from the sale of these few copies than would have been realized if the entire edition had been sold at its regular price.[12] After 1872, by decision of the council of ministers, two copies of each banned book had to be deposited in the secret section of the public library. The most complete collection is now in the Saltykov-Shchedrin Public Library in Leningrad.[13]

In assessing the nature and effects of literary censorship in tsarist Russia, one should bear in mind that extremely harsh measures on the part of the government seem to have been the rule rather than the exception when the government was reacting to uprisings or revolutions, real or imaginary, either at home or abroad. Yet nineteenth-century Russia produced some of the world's greatest literature, despite the fact that virtually every writer at one time or another had his bouts with the censor. The instances where either Catherine II or Nicholas I acted as censor were rare. For the most part censors were available to writers or editors who wished to argue their cases before them. Sometimes the censor was himself an author and, as in the case of Ivan Goncharov, censored his own novels. Tsarist censorship of the nineteenth century may have banned certain topics, but it did not specify what a writer had to write or how he had to write it. The claim has often been made that the very existence of some form of censorship created a great literature, because writers had to be clever enough to bypass obstacles and still transmit the message they wished to convey.

[12] Ibid., p. 17.
[13] Ibid., p. 24.

The voluminous literature describing aspects of censorship in tsarist Russia which was published in Russia at the time censorship was in effect and the more recent studies by Soviet scholars who have been most eager to point up the deficiencies of the tsarist government provide us with an abundance of data for the tsarist period, but for the Soviet period documentation is limited. The Soviet claim is that the October Revolution did away with censorship, except for military emergencies; that the Soviet Constitution guarantees a free press[14] which is true to the extent that there is no officially listed post of censor. Instead, the functions of the censor are performed by Glavlit (the Chief Administration for Literature and Publications). In actual fact a number of other agencies and individuals are concerned with censorship, including the leaders of the Soviet Union.

What we know of the Soviet censorship system is derived from accounts given by former Soviet citizens who in one way or another had direct experience with the process of censorship, primarily in regard to the Soviet press,[15] from analyses of literary

[14] The following statement from the Great Soviet Encyclopedia may be taken as official: "The Great October Socialist Revolution put an end to both Tsarist and bourgeois censorship. . . . Censorship in the USSR has a completely different character than that in the bourgeois states. It is an organ of the socialist state, its activity is directed towards the protection of the miliatry and state press, and also towards the prevention of the publication of materials which can do harm to the interests of the workers. The constitution of the USSR, statute 125, guarantees all workers freedom of the press, which means guaranteed access to print, a supply of paper, and other material conditions." *Bol'shaja sovetskaja entsiklopedija*, 2nd ed., 51 vols. (Moscow, 1950–1958), 46: 518.

[15] Discussion of the mechanics of Soviet press and literary censorship is derived principally from three such accounts. Arkadij Gerasimovich Gaev, *Tsenzura sovetskoj pechati, Issledodovanija i materialy*, series 2,

works which were banned or changed as a result of criticism, and from statements about censorship made by writers in the Soviet Union, particularly within the past decade. While it may be many years before any definitive statements can be made about the nature of literary censorship in the USSR, the outlines of the system are clear. Soviet censorship regulations are a part of a state system characterized by complete centralization and by the establishment of strictly defined frameworks in all spheres of life. A full picture of the censorship system as it relates to the press, but also to a certain extent for belles lettres, in descending order of importance is as follows: (1) the party head; (2) the Praesidium of the Central Committee of the Party (formerly the Politburo of the Central Committee); (3) the Kremlin's press department; (4) the press department of the Central Committee of the Communist Party of the Soviet Union; (5) the editorial board of newspapers and magazines; (6) the editorial staff; (7) Glavlit. Thus the office which nominally carries out censorship functions (Glavlit) is really the junior body. High executives in the party and the government have more control over the daily press than members of Glavlit who are simply state security employees without jurisdiction in questions of prime importance; they simply carry out instructions.

A brief description of how Soviet press censorship works can lead to a better understanding of some of the processes to which the belles lettres are subjected. For newspaper publication, an article is shown to the chief of section or to a member of the edito-

---

no. 23 (Munich: Institute for the Study of the History and Culture of the USSR, 1955); Kajkhosro Kipiani, "Sovetskaja tsenzura," *Nashi Dni,* no. 6 (1959), pp. 28–38; M. Koriakov, "Soviets Lie About Censorship," *U.S. News and World Report* 40 (January 13, 1956), 68–74.

rial board. He makes suggestions, and the article is rewritten. Then it goes to a "responsible secretary" of the editorial board, a kind of managing editor. Upon his approval, it goes to the print shop. The galley proofs are read by the deputy chief editor and included in the dummy of the paper. Page proof is then read by no fewer than six "responsible workers": the department head, the responsible secretary, the deputy editor, the night editor, the editor in chief, almost all of whom are party members, and then the political editor, the real and final censor. Only after the latter has affixed his code number signifying his approval at the bottom of the last page can any Soviet paper or book be printed.

The article is checked for things that are not supposed to be mentioned. Censors all have handbooks, but they are closely guarded, and apparently none have found their way to the West, or at least none have been published there. Soviet newspapers print nothing about train wrecks, although they do happen; nothing about plane crashes, unless on someone else's territory; no mention of leper colonies or hospitals for lepers in the USSR, or of unemployment, venereal disease, or prostitution—as if not mentioning them means they do not exist. Above all, except in the columns of *samokritika* (self-criticism), the press is required to be optimistic. In agricultural publications, for example, crop failures, hailstorms, or disasters cannot be mentioned. The censors also scrutinize through a magnifying glass all drawings and photographs for any symbol or sign that could have some political meaning. For example, in an agricultural publication, a diagram of a harvester with a device to pick up grain that would otherwise be wasted showed two lines crossed in such a way as to suggest a swastika to the censor; the diagram had to be removed.

In the early Soviet period, through the 1920's and to the time of the first Five-Year Plan, the organs of Soviet censorship, whatever they may have been at the time, permitted the publication of all kinds of literature, in a variety of literary styles, provided that the literature was not opposed to the policies of the regime at that time. By 1934, however, when the official style of "socialist realism" was put into effect, when all of the smaller, experimental, somewhat independent literary groups were done away with, when the Union of Soviet Writers was established, the government had effectively taken control over artistic literature in the same way that it had always controlled the daily press. It was no longer possible, as a writer, simply not to be opposed to the regime. Now one had to support the regime, and one had to be optimistic.

Solzhenitsyn, in *The Cancer Ward*, delineates the impossible task faced by the Soviet writers, in a conversation between Rusanov's daughter and a patient in the hospital:

"So, you fellow, try to understand. It is much easier to describe things as they are than to describe what does not yet exist but what you know will come about. What we see with our bare eyes today is not necessarily the real truth. Truth is what *ought* to be, what will come about tomorrow. And we have to describe our wonderful tomorrow."

"Then tomorrow what will they describe?" The confused boy wrinkled his brow.

"Tomorrow? Tomorrow they'll describe the after-tomorrow. Looking ahead."[16]

In dealing with artistic literature, with literary criticism, and

16 Solzhenitsyn, *The Cancer Ward*, p. 337.

with the Soviet versions of the so-called fat or thick journals, chief responsibility for ensuring that the book or article does in fact correspond to the political and cultural demands of the time (or the proper rendition of the tomorrow), rests with the editorial staff of the journal or publishing house. It is impractical to have a preliminary reading of all manuscripts by someone higher up in the government, although eventually every book does have such an evaluation.

In the Soviet Union, writers literally do have to think in terms of what tomorrow will bring, because the manuscript written at a particular time may already be outdated by the time it is scheduled for publication. The author, especially if he is a young or inexperienced author, probably first consults with some of the senior authors in the appropriate section of the Union of Soviet Writers even before submitting the manuscript to the editor of a journal or to a publishing house.

The editor of a journal gives it to consultants who may suggest changes, then to a member of his staff, and finally he may present it to the board of the journal in question. Publication in a journal or in book form, usually in a relatively small edition, is then followed by criticism in selected newspapers and periodicals. *Pravda* and *Izvestija* generally refrain from any precipitous commentary and may not comment at all, but if they do, then the entire critical apparatus of the country must follow suit. A novelist must make recommended changes before his work can be published again. Prior to 1950 or so, the reader was never told that the novel had been revised.

One exception to this was Alexander Fadeev's novel, *The Young Guard* (1945), a novel which presumably had been based on most extensive documentation. The novel appeared serially in *The Banner* and the *Komsomol Pravda* between 1943 and 1945.[17] The plot is based on documentary evidence gathered by the Central Committee of the Komsomol and given to Fadeev. Fadeev visited the Krasnodon area himself, questioned the people there, and only then proceeded with his writing. The story was a true story about a group of young people who successfully harassed the Germans in the occupation zone, but who were caught eventually and killed. Fadeev was awarded a Stalin Prize for the work. It was made into a play and a movie and enjoyed unprecedented acclaim both in the Soviet Union and abroad.[18] Two years after its publication the novel was suddenly criticized in *Pravda* on the ground that the old Bolsheviks in the novel, who had been left behind to lead the underground opposition, but who, according to Fadeev, had in fact been captured by the Germans quite early, had not been portrayed correctly. Fadeev was asked to show more clearly the leadership role of these old Bolsheviks.[19]

We do not, of course, have the documentary evidence to prove that Fadeev was correct in the original version, or that the critic in *Pravda* was correct, but nevertheless, four years later, in 1951, Fadeev did produce a revised version of his novel, which was immediately acclaimed by his colleagues and by party officials. In this case an open declaration may have been necessary, because the party itself was reversing its previous stand and because the story was already so well known to most Soviet citizens, who had either read the novel or seen a stage adaptation of it.[20]

[17] Aleksandr Fadeev, *Molodaja Gvardija, Znamja,* and *Komsomol'-skaja Pravda* (Moscow, 1943–1945).

[18] K. Zelinskij, "A. Fadeev," *Novyj Mir* 2 (Moscow, 1947): 190.

[19] *Pravda,* Dec. 3, 1947.

[20] For a fuller discussion of the problems involved see Vera Aleksandrova, "Chistjat vernejshikh, *Sotsialisticheskij Vestnik* 1 (New York,

In another instance, this one not publicized, a less well known writer, V. Kostylev, was criticized for his presentation of Ivan the Terrible in his novel of the same title when it appeared in one of the fat journals, *October*, in 1942. Kostylev responded to the criticism and proved that he was correct, but in the end he changed his novel to fit the criticism.[21]

In still another instance on record of a highly placed party official who was responsible for the demise of a writer, Andrei Zhdanov, then the party hack in matters of literature, attacked Mikhail Zoshchenko, one of the most popular humorists in the Soviet Union, but unfortunately also a man who had run afoul of the party bureaucracy on a number of occasions. In 1946 Zoshchenko had published a long short story entitled *Adventures of an Ape*, presumably a children's story. This was the story of a monkey who had escaped from the zoo after it had been bombed during the war. At first the monkey enjoyed his freedom, but then everywhere he went little boys kept chasing him and harassing him. In the end he came to the conclusion that life in the zoo was really better for him than life out in the world. Zhdanov said the implication of the story was clear: It was better to live in a zoo than in Soviet society. As a result of this criticism Zoshchenko was dismissed from the Union of Soviet Writers, and consequently for two or three years denied the right to publish in the Soviet Union.[22]

1948): 15–16 and "Posmertnye ispytanija [Molodoj gvardii]," *Sotsialisticheskij Vestnik* 1–2 (1952); 21–23.

[21] For full details see my article, "A Novel in Flux: V. Kostylev's *Ivan Groznyj*," *The American Slavic and East European Review* 14 (October 1955): 359–370.

[22] See Rebecca A. Domar, "The Tragedy of a Soviet Satirist, or the Case of Zoshchenko," in *Through the Glass of Soviet Literature*, ed.,

No discussion of censorship can be complete without at least mentioning Boris Pasternak's novel *Doctor Zhivago* and its fate at the hands of the editorial board of the liberal journal *New World*. The manuscript of *Doctor Zhivago* was held up by the editorial board of the journal, and only after Pasternak had been awarded the Nobel Prize did the board find it necessary to indicate why the novel had been rejected for publication. Interestingly enough, the letter of rejection discussed openly, for all of Soviet society to see, those very passages which presumably made it impossible to publish the novel. There is some basis then for support of Max Hayward's assertion that *Doctor Zhivago* was not published in the Soviet Union because Alexei Surkov, then Secretary of the Writers' Union, disliked Pasternak and was able to prevent publication.[23]

The foregoing examples show that high party officials can and do act as censors, but on the other hand we must consider that these same officials are also the only ones who can make abrupt changes in the official party line. This is what happened in the case of Alexander Solzhenitsyn's short novel, *One Day in the Life of Ivan Denisovich*, which describes a day in one of the notorious labor camps of the far north. Alexander Tvardovsky, editor of the *New World*, sent it to Khrushchev, who wanted to use it as a weapon in his power struggle with the hard-liners Mikhail Suslov and Frol Kozlov. According to one report, Khrushchev had twen-

---

Ernest J. Simmons (New York: Columbia University Press, 1953), 201–243. An excellent summary of "Zhdanovism" is presented in Walter N. Vickery, "Zhdanovism (1946–1953)" in *Literature and Revolution in Soviet Russia 1917–1962*, a symposium edited by Max Hayward and Leopold Labedz (London: Oxford University Press, 1963), pp. 99–124.

[23] Max Hayward, "Zhivago's Suppression: A New Theory," *Library Journal* 84 (May 15, 1959), 1562–1563.

ty copies run off on the Kremlin press and distributed to members
of the Praesidium. The Praesidium met at Khrushchev's request.
Each member sat at a long table with a copy of the book. Khrushchev came in. He was greeted by silence. Khrushchev said, "Com-
rades, it's a good book, isn't it?" Still no one spoke. At which
point he said, "There's a Russian proverb, 'Silence gives con-
sent.' " He strode out. Actually the silence did not last. There was
considerable controversy in the Soviet hierarchy, but, on Khrushchev's direct authorization, the book was published and appeared
in the November 1962 issue of *New World*.[24]

Since that time, the world has witnessed a series of events unprecedented in the Soviet Union, including the trial of several
young writers who were convicted of anti-Soviet activity. Among
these young writers were Andrei Sinyavsky (Abram Tertz) and
Julii Daniel (Nikolai Arzhak), who were tried in February of
1967 and sentenced respectively to seven and five years at hard
labor. Other young writers have been sentenced for similar activity. At least four writers have been declared insane. One, Valery
Tarsis, is now in the United States.

In 1967, for the first time, there was open, publicized demand
to abolish censorship. In May of that year Solzhenitsyn sent to
the members of the Fourth Congress of Soviet Writers his ap-
peal for the abolition of literary censorship in the USSR. In his
letter he implicated the Writers' Union for failing to defend the
legitimate rights of its members, including "protection of copy-
right" and the "protection of other rights of writers." He referred
to the interdictions and persecutions to which he had been subjected—the ban against the publication of his works, the un-

[24] "Writer's Pen Should Not Be Stopped: Excerpts from a Letter by
A. Solzhenitsyn," *Time Magazine*, Sept. 27, 1968, pp. 22–27.

authorized publication of other works in "closed editions" for "reading by a select unidentified circle," the confiscation of his manuscripts, personal papers, and literary archives, the slander and abuse directed against him, and the ban against the public reading of his works.

Solzhenitsyn received considerable support from the literary and intellectual community in the USSR, but the real indication of who is winning in this struggle is clear. Solzhenitsyn was expelled from the Writers' Union in November 1969, and in February 1970 Tvardovsky, who had long been the editor of the *New World*, was removed from his post.[25]

Young writers today who cannot be published in the official press turn increasingly to the facilities of the so-called *samizdat* (self-publishing house). Thousands of typewriters in the Soviet Union are being used to type an original and four or five carbons of a particular work of literature. Someone else makes additional copies and so it goes. Printing presses, mimeograph machines, even ditto machines would be suspect, but large numbers of people can and do own typewriters. Since they are all of the same make, it is difficult for the secret police to track down any one particular machine, and so the process goes on. Two of Solzhenitsyn's novels, *The Cancer Ward* and *The First Circle*, which were denied publication in the USSR, found their way to the

[25] Solzhenitsyn's letter to the Writers' Congress was never published in the Soviet Union, but copies were circulated, and these evoked a response from many Soviet writers who joined in a campaign in his support. Several interesting documents in the original Russian and in English translation have been compiled by the Radio Liberty Committee. See "More About Solzhenitsyn," *Radio Liberty Dispatch* (New York: Jan. 1968), 18 pages.

West in just this way, apparently contrary to Solzhenitsyn's wishes.[26]

In summary, the tradition of official literary censorship in Russia is of long duration. There is no question but that censorship under the Soviets over the past forty years has been much more pervasive and controlled than it ever was in nineteenth- and twentieth-century tsarist Russia. Any number of Soviet officials today have the kind of power over the fate of writers that once could be held only by the head of state.

In the nineteenth century authors were told only of the topics they could not discuss. The Soviet list of forbidden topics is a much longer one, and, in addition, the author is told what he must write about and how he must write it, in conformity with the official style of Socialist Realism.

Great works of literature were written and published in tsarist Russia at the time censorship was in force, but almost none in the Soviet Union since 1930. Most of those few have been published abroad rather than in the Soviet Union. Whether or not there exists somewhere in the USSR a stock of manuscripts of the high caliber of Mikhail A. Bulgakov's *The Master and Margarita*, a genuine masterpiece written from 1928 to 1940 but published in the USSR only in 1966–1967, is not known.

To hope that the Soviets will relinquish their control over the press and artistic literature is unrealistic. A totalitarian system requires, above all, control of the channels of communication, in order to retain power. Only a change in regime or the passage of time will make it possible to write studies of Soviet censorship comparable to the ones we now have for the tsarist period.

[26] Albert Parry, "Samizdat is Russia's Underground Press," the *New York Times*, Magazine Section, March 15, 1970, pp. 64–77.

The admirable struggle of the intellectuals in the Soviet Union, the underground literary journals, the home industry of publication by typewriter may, of course, bring some of the very best writing to the West where it can be published, but the leading writers almost inevitably will be apprehended or they will not have the energy and the willpower to continue writing and publishing without financial recompense. Authors writing for the underground publications do not receive any compensation, and, if their works are published abroad, they are not permitted to collect any royalties. Financially, then, they are at a distinct disadvantage vis-à-vis the Soviet writer who publishes through regular channels. The underground writer can, in fact, never be a full-time writer, because he must have some other job to earn a livelihood.

So, despite the old proverb, "Once you have joined the pack, even if you do not bark, the least you can do is to wag your tail," in the nineteenth and early twentieth century you did not really have to join a pack, or bark, or wag. You could even bark against the pack and still survive, though it might be unpleasant. But under the Soviets, even if you do not want to join, you must bark or wag with vigor.